HIRA MANDI

Claudine Le Tourneur d'Ison became a freelance journalist after studying Literature, History of Art and Egyptology in Paris. She works for French media, television and has published twelve books, biographies, travel books and novels. She has been travelling all over the world and developed a great passion for Indian Subcontinent and Asia.

OTHER INDIAINK TITLES

Anjana Basu	*Black Tongue*
Anjana Basu	*Chinku and the Wolfboy*
Anjum Hasan	*Neti, Neti*
Anuradha Majumdar	*Infinity Paper: A mysterious quest, an unforgettable adventure*
A.N.D. Haksar	*Madhav & Kama: A Love Story from Ancient India*
Boman Desai	*Servant, Master, Mistress*
Chitra Banerjee Divakaruni	*Shadowland*
C.P. Surendran	*An Iron Harvest*
Haider Warraich	*The Auras of the Jinn*
I. Allan Sealy	*The Everest Hotel*
I. Allan Sealy	*Trotternama*
Indrajit Hazra	*The Garden of Earthly Delights*
Jaspreet Singh	*17 Tomatoes: Tales from Kashmir*
Jawahara Saidullah	*The Burden of Foreknowledge*
John MacLithon	*Hindutva, Sex & Adventure*
Kalpana Swaminathan	*The Page 3 Murders*
Kalpana Swaminathan	*The Gardener's Song*
Kamalini Sengupta	*The Top of the Raintree*
Lavanya Shanbaoug	*An Imperial Friend*
Madhavan Kutty	*The Village Before Time*
Pankaj Mishra	*The Romantics*
Paro Anand	*Pure Sequence*
Rakesh Satyal	*Blue Boy*
Ranjit Lal	*Bambi Chops and Wags*
Ranjit Lal	*The Life &Times of Altu-Faltu*
Ranjit Lal	*The Small Tigers of Shergarh*
Ranjit Lal	*The Simians of South Block and Yumyum Piglets*
Raza Mir & Ali Husain Mir	*Anthems of Resistance: A Celebration of Progressive Urdu Poetry*
Sanjay Bahadur	*The Sound of Water*
Sanjay Bahadur	*Hul: Cry Rebel!*
Selina Sen	*A Mirror Greens in Spring*
Shandana Minhas	*Tunnel Vision*
Sharmistha Mohanty	*New Life*
Shree Ghatage	*Brahma's Dream*
Sudhir Thapliyal	*Crossing the Road*
Susan Visvanathan	*Nelycinda and Other Stories*
Susan Visvanathan	*The Visiting Moon*
Susan Visvanathan	*The Seine at Noon*
Tanushree Podder	*Escape from Harem*

HIRA MANDI

Claudine Le Tourneur d'Ison

Translated from French

Priyanka Jhijaria

First published in English in 2012
Second impression, 2017
IndiaInk
An imprint of
Roli Books Pvt. Ltd
M-75, Greater Kailash II Market
New Delhi 110 048
Phone: ++91 (011) 4068 2000
Fax: ++91 (011) 2921 7185
E-mail: info@rolibooks.com; Website: www.rolibooks.com

Also at
Bangalore, Chennai, & Mumbai

Cover: Akhila Sethi

ISBN: 978-81-86939-54-3

Typeset in Bembo by Roli Books Pvt. Ltd
printed at Repro India Ltd., Mumbai.
Published in association with the French Embassy in India

To

Late Iqbal Mustafa,

my dearest friend in Pakistan

PROLOGUE

Alone in front of his house, Shanwaz doesn't see the crowd that rushes up as the wind sends the first flames up into the sky. All the neighbours spill into the street shouting '*Pani! Pani!*', 'Water! Water!'. But where would they find abundant water in this old, decrepit city? Kindled by the gentle north wind, the fire feasts on the dry wood of the *mashrabiahs* – the lattice-worked Mughal door, and the balconies with their carved golden flowers. Crackling gleefully, the indescribably sensual flames dance and swirl around the jambs, devouring the story of an entire life as they reach into the night.

1

Shanwaz Nadeem's first memory was a distant one, of being awoken every night by the creaking of the heavy entrance door, when he was a child. He had soon understood that it meant his mother had come home from work. What happened so close to him after that, just on the other side of the partition in the room decorated with plastic flowers and pink curtains, was a mystery to him. The moans, the sighs and cries that he heard were both intriguing and frightening. His mother was not alone. He wanted to cry, and he curled up on his mattress on the floor in the dark night, waiting for the unbearable confusion of these noises to end. He knew that once she was alone, she would gently push open the door to his room. He would then make out her tall silhouette like a shadow puppet bending over him to see that he was sleeping well. As always, he would pretend to be fast asleep.

When his eyes opened early in the mornings, the house resonated with a silence only barely broken by the birds chirping in the cluster of trees on the small square just behind the house. The sun filtered through panels of coloured glass in his room, dappling the wooden floor with warm oranges and yellows. He would lie there on the floor with only two toys ever given to him, a small *tonga* – like the wooden horse-driven carts that cruised the alleys of Lahore, and a stuffed toy that didn't look like any of the animals he saw outside. He would sit the animal down in the cart and push the two around on the floor for hours on end. From time to time he would lean out of the narrow window and observe the street below. But in this area, everything was still engulfed in deep sleep in the morning. Doors remained closed and curtains drawn. As though, however hard it tried, the sun was unable to pull this part of the city out of the abyss of the night.

His mother was called Naseem. A name that sounded like music to his child's ears. As soon as he heard her move on the other side of the wall, he would stop playing and stand transfixed, attentively listening to the rustling that accompanied each slow step of her difficult awakening to the world. And when the door to his room finally opened, he would run to her, enveloping her calves in his five-year-old arms, relieved to be with her and to have her to himself after such a long wait. Naseem would pick him up and hold him to her breast, tenderly kissing him and talking to him. Nothing pleased Shanwaz more than these all-too-fleeting moments that left him breathless with sadness when his mother let go of him so quickly, and put him back on the floor as she went to make tea in the cubbyhole which served as a kitchen. His eyes would fill with tears at the thought of waiting again for the next day to inhale the soft perfume of her long black hair.

Naseem and Shanwaz lived on the second floor of the old Mughal house that had belonged to Naseem's mother. It was falling into disrepair for lack of funds – the floorboards were worm-eaten, the doors were barely hanging on to their hinges, humidity seeped through the walls, the curtains on the windows were slowly rotting and the bitter smell of decay and mildew filled the air. Sometimes Shanwaz surprised a rat passing through the gaps in the wood. He thought it was fun – it was a rare distraction in the never-ending days he spent by himself. The school was too far away, beyond the walls of the old city. Naseem could not afford to send him there. For Shanwaz, his mother's room was the most beautiful part of the house, the only one she had been obliged to restore and do up, if but a little. She had put a real bed in there instead of a mattress on the floor, like most of the inhabitants of the area. Then she had gone across town to the most fashionable neighbourhood where all the rich women came to shop – the infernally tempting Anarkali bazaar, a paradise of shops, each more inviting than the other. It was all too expensive for Naseem, but she had wanted the best to make the room luxurious and comfortable. After all, it was where most of her income came from. After much hesitation, she had finally bought several metres of a silky fabric in candy pink for the curtains and the bed cover. She had also found heart-shaped cushions which she covered in the same fabric and the obscure room became bright and inviting. After a lengthy discussion with a furniture seller in Kashmiri bazaar, she negotiated a reasonable price for a pretty dresser with a mirror to admire her slim twenty-year-old silhouette in. Electricity hadn't yet reached the old Mughal city, so she lit lanterns in the evenings – she needed the soft sensual intimate air the orange light lent to her room. Shanwaz was obsessed by this atmosphere. It was not meant for him. As soon as he was alone, he would go and snuggle deep into the cushions, sniffing for traces of the precious smell of his mother's neck that intoxicated him every morning. For the rest of his life, that smell of jasmine mixed with musk would remain one of his most evocative memories of a woman.

Since her mother's death, Naseem shared the house with her two aunts and their daughters who lived on the first and third floors. On the last floor, the roof was a large terrace overlooking the Badshahi mosque. At sunset the women liked to gather there to enjoy the only open space, especially in the summer when it became so humid in the house that there was nothing to do but lie in bed. It was an ordeal to wear even the finest cotton on glistening sweaty skin. Summer was real torture for women because they were obliged to leave the house covered from head to toe, veiled in the folds of their saris.

Shanwaz was the only man of the family. As a child he was always the object of gentle kisses, caresses, and tender words. In the afternoons, once the women finally awoke, the house resembled a bird market. They hopped from floor to floor, twirled around on the stairs, and jabbered endlessly. His greedy eyes would spy on these girls, only a little younger than his mother, their doll-like faces and fiery black eyes, long hair left loose on their narrow shoulders when at home, their graceful gestures, the seductive elegance of their smiles, and the spontaneity they lost as soon as evening came.

Compared to his beguiling cousins who completely fascinated him, Naseem's two aunts seemed very old to him. Most of all, Shanwaz felt, they had no joy left in their eyes and he was struck by it whenever they looked at him. Even their smiles were not real smiles with pretty white teeth. When their lips parted, he was horror-struck by the huge black holes where stumps of teeth waded in red mucousy juice. He was also amazed at their corpulence – their flesh was no longer confined within their cotton clothes, but flowed out in fat lumps wherever it could find a gap. And they were also rude with him. Never a kind word, always scolding. When his mother was out, they made him do household chores. He would often pretend not to hear when they called his name.

'Shanwaz! Shanwaz! Come here!' they yelled, and their voices made his hairs stand on end.

He would hide in his room, waiting, knowing full well that he would not have the upper hand. Sooner or later, the aunts would send up the poor, skinny servant girl who was as petrified as he was. With no other choice left, he would go down to the first floor where the two shrews had set up house in indescribable chaos, steeped in the stink of old women who forget to empty their bucket of excreta into the street gutters in the morning. They would hand him a few rupees and send him to the other end of the town to buy something he could just as easily have found right next to the house. They always hoped that he would lose his way and never come back.

And that was generally what happened – he *would* get lost. He could hardly find his way around the neighbourhood, let alone the other end of the town … a labyrinth of dirty streets, dilapidated houses, alleys spilling forth their miasma, walls oozing the sickness of time, carved wooden balconies labouring, by Allah's grace, to remain suspended over the streets where life was bursting in its most primitive form; yet this enigmatic, miserable world was also the most hospitable. When the shopkeepers sitting cross-legged in their stalls saw the little cherub swallowing his fear at all costs and heading out, they showed him the way and gave him fruit or a few sweets as he went by. With the help of his horrid aunts, he learned to find his way around and discovered the world around him.

When he got back home, he would hand over the goods and the change hoping they would give him a little something, but they never did. His mother, though, was more generous. He stashed his kitty inside his stuffed toy's belly by undoing a few centimetres of the stitches, just enough to hide a few coins. In the late afternoons, he listened fervently for the street vendor's refrain. He would rush up to the window and lower a wicker basket at the end of a string with money inside it, and the man would place Shanwaz's favourite mango-flavoured ice cream stick inside. Sweet respite! A moment of pure delight. He would forget his loneliness, his mother's cries in the night, and the squalid odours of the house, and with a clear head, concentrate on the cold, juicy pulp melting more quickly in his hands than in his mouth. But he never lost a drop of it. He would lick clean every little finger and palm where sugary remains were lodged, then lie down on the floor and close his eyes to savour the last traces of mango on his taste buds before drifting off to sleep.

When he opened his eyes, the day had ended. His mother was by his side, sitting cross-legged in front of their dinner – piping hot rotis that she had prepared herself, with spicy vegetables and sometimes, meat. Outside, the air was electric. The heat buzzed like a swarm of bees. Even the evenings weren't cool. Naseem didn't eat much. Her soft face became closed at night. Her eyes left for other places, in another world. She was no longer accessible. He would stare at her. She would emerge and smile at him, but the smile was quickly lost in a sort of faraway melancholy which he knew he wasn't a part of. Soon she would kiss him, get up, disappear into her room and leave him standing there with a knot in his throat and tears slipping out from under his thick lashes. His mind was full of shapeless thoughts and torturous ideas that were not easily expressed in words.

When Naseem reappeared, his heart beat wildly, awed by the splendour of the woman before him draped in a magnificent blue silk sari with jewels around her ankles, her wrists and her neck, heavy ear-rings dangling from her ears, her face so made up that she suddenly appeared much older than she was and more fiercely beautiful.

'Be good. I won't be late,' she would say as she left. Her scarlet mouth would open to reveal her snowy-white teeth. He never got used to the spectacle of her dressed up like this, and every evening he would find himself under the spell of this woman who aroused bizarre sensations in the pit of his stomach. Then she would disappear, and he could hear her in the stairwell, leaving with her cousins who were also all dressed up, and the two aunts who rolled their elephantine derrières down the worm-eaten stairs. They all went off into the night. Where did they go? Of course, his mother had never hidden from him that she was a dancer. But where did she dance? For whom? In the shadows of the house – Naseem always left an oil lamp burning close to the stairs – he crept up to his mother's room. It was perfectly tidy and clean, with a strong, nauseating smell that clung to the air and permeated everything. A tub filled with water stood in a corner with a towel hanging by. Was his mother going to wash herself when she got back? An obscure pain twisted his bowels as he stood there surrounded by a world full of secrets he did not have access to. Something told him that what happened on this provocative pink bed full of strange smells that his mother had so painstakingly made welcoming and gay, took away a little of her youth every day. He became certain of it when he saw her emerge from an abyss of nightmares one afternoon, her face all shrivelled up, and indescribable sadness in the depths of her gloomy, swollen eyes. She was ageing prematurely like the other women in the family. Would she end up looking like the aunts? No! He refused to believe it.

One night he was awakened with a start by a man's rumbling voice on the other side of the partition. He heard a thumping on the floorboards, then Naseem's feeble voice. He crouched on his mattress, clutching the sheet in his two hands, incapable of any movement, trembling as though an icy wind had swept over him. A violent argument had broken out. When he heard the man hit his mother and heard her cry out, he was up in a bound to go to her rescue. What he saw behind the door remained forever engraved in his memories. A half-naked Naseem with her sari in tatters was trying to push away the monster above her with her skinny arms, while he held her neck down with one hand and the other, high in the air, moved down to strike her head.

'No! No!' Shanwaz screamed, throwing himself on the man and grabbing hold of his trousers with all his force to pull him out of the room.

Taken aback, the angry man didn't immediately understand what was happening. Then, abashed, he had let go, straightened his clothes and snarled, 'I'll kill you, filthy whore!' as he left the room.

Shanwaz had looked at his mother in fright. She was bleeding from the mouth and huge stains had mottled the bedspread, making strange flowers on the pink. Naseem had pulled her son into her arms, hugged him close to her, crying softly, 'Oh, Shanwaz! Shanwaz!'

For two days and two nights, Naseem watched over her son and held a wet cloth to his forehead. The child was possessed with a fever that made his eyes roll about in his head like marbles. The aunts had a concoction prepared from herbs bought in the intriguing healers' neighbourhood, the Bazaar-e-Hakimah, a world of extraordinarily persuasive beady-eyed sellers of vials full of terrifying mysteries. By the grace of God, the child recovered by the third day and Naseem went back to her nocturnal activities.

As soon as winter ended, Shanwaz would leave his room and spend entire days on the roof. The cold that iced his veins in the humid house was finally leaving the city. A warm wind was bringing in a bit of white into the too-blue sky of the past months. It was the most magical time of the year, as though after a long hibernation, a sudden explosion of energy had gushed out of the earth's innards to renew the blood of all Lahoris. To mark this return to life, all the inhabitants of the old Mughal city would gather on the rooftops on the first day of spring to celebrate *Basant*, the kite festival.

In the early morning, after the muezzin's call, men, women, and children would throw the majestic rustling silk butterflies up towards the silvery sun and watch them open their gigantic wings out in the sky. Until evening, Lahore was a kaleidoscope of multi-coloured dots. Shanwaz would hang on to his kite, exhilarated. Far above him flew the strange bird he called out names to, identifying with it to the point of imagining it was he that was high up, blown away by the wind towards absolute liberty. Around him, women prepared the traditional Basant meal, and in the evening, when the blood-red sun disappeared between the two minarets of the Badshahi, bringing on the night as fast as an extinguished lamp, the men lit torches everywhere. The thousands of little lights clung to the sky, and the city seemed to float in the air like a giant ship on an inky sea.

A few months later, Shanwaz, who always observed his mother with great care, noticed a slight change in her usually svelte silhouette. Her stomach protruded slightly, round as a ball under the sari. When she held him in her arms, he could feel a firm, compact roundness against him, and it was such a strange sensation that he sometimes imagined his mother metamorphosing into something like one of the aunts whose bellies had taken on monstrous proportions. She stopped going out with the cousins in the evenings and stayed back with him. He was so happy that he started liking the ball that was getting increasingly big and, in a way, becoming responsible for their new life. His mother all to himself for days on end – he'd never known more happiness. He couldn't care any longer if she became as fat as the aunts. In fact, the bigger her belly became, the more she held him close, took care of him and loved him. Shanwaz was wallowing in a sense of well-being that he would soon not know for a long time to come. But for now he was unaware of it, and enjoyed the giddy sensuality and voluptuousness of this relationship he believed to be eternal.

One day, he was awoken by loud cries. Someone had locked him inside his room. From the other side he could hear an unusual flurry of activity, women's voices, his cousins. He banged on the door with clenched fists, screeching his lungs out, 'Let me out! I want to come out! Ma! Open the door! Ma!'

But no one took heed of his cries. He sat sobbing on the floor for hours, then suddenly panicked when he understood that it was his mother who was wailing like an animal. He cried out again, beating as hard as he could against the partition wall, convinced in his childish despair that his mother was being throttled.

When the door finally opened, through a veil of tears he saw one of his cousins flash him a dazzling smile. She leaned towards him and took him by the hand, 'Come! Your mother has a gift for you!' Exhausted but relieved at the thought that his mother was alive, he quietly entered the room where the family was. She sat there in the middle of the bed with a tiny baby nestled in her arms. Where had this child come from? 'Come closer,' she murmured to him.

Sweat was running down her unrecognisable face. It had lost all its colour and glow.

'Come, come closer. Come and kiss your sister Laila.'

Sister? How was this possible? He froze, unbelieving at the foot of the bed. He was totally confused.

But his cousins and aunts raised an unbearable ruckus and forced him to kiss the child.

It took some time for Shanwaz to understand what had happened. His life changed in one fell swoop. So this was the reason behind his mother's round belly, this incessantly wiggling, whining gnome that everyone in the family worshipped as though it were a treasure, the key to all joys, and for whom he was totally and permanently abandoned.

With Laila's arrival, everybody's daily routine was disrupted for months. In this neighbourhood of fatherless children, a woman's only dream was to give birth to as many girls as possible to perpetuate their dancers' lineage. While the birth of a girl child was seen almost as a miracle, a boy child was generally welcomed with a funeral lament. This was what Shanwaz had come to understand. And he was embittered by the disregard with which he was now treated.

When Laila turned four, Naseem bought her a pretty pink sari and anklets with little bells for her feet. She called in a musician to play the harmonium while the little one twisted and twirled, imitating her mother who danced with her. Laila was very graceful and showed a real aptitude for dance. The mellow glances she threw at her public left no doubt of her talent, and warmed the hearts of all the brothel females.

Shanwaz sat by himself in a corner and watched her, entranced by this child he had at first violently rejected and ardently detested. Now he was captivated by this little chit of a woman. She appeased his pain of being alive and aimless, and about to turn ten.

2

Shanwaz never forgot the year he turned ten. Or the bloody inferno the country was plunged into, or the unbelievable insanity of adults one August morning in 1947.

A bomb exploded near the Bhati Gate cinema hall, rousing the entire neighbourhood. Houses trembled, and people came running out into the streets. Shanwaz went tearing down the streets and dived into one leading up to Bhati Gate. The closer he got, the more the compact morning crowd seemed horrified, the inhabitants dishevelled and weary-eyed as though they had met the devil in person. It became more and more difficult for him to make his way through and when he finally arrived close to the cinema, the building had a big gaping hole in it. Bits and pieces of torn, agonizing humans lay everywhere. He was left rooted to the spot in horror. Policemen arrived, pushing out those who were trying to help the victims. Tongas were roped in to carry the wounded to hospitals while the dead – fifty Muslims – were lined up along a pavement. Men were shouting 'Vengeance! Vengeance!' An hour later, not far from there, a hundred-and-fifty Hindus were massacred with knives and their houses were burned down.

The Partition of India had begun.

In the old city, people didn't dare come out of their houses in the evenings any more. They remained holed up at home, and they all gave up the old Punjabi custom of sleeping on the roofs for fear of sabres that appeared out of nowhere in the dark. At the height of the terror Naseem and her cousins stopped receiving clients. The heavy entrance door was locked every night. Prayers of mourning and grief filled the nights – 'Allah ho Akbar' on one side, 'Sat Sri Akal' on the other, while fires continued to light up the night sky. The police went around the city imposing a curfew. Shanwaz could no longer sleep well. Images of the carnage came back to haunt him incessantly. Blood, the purple flaming river of man's hate, the dark liquid with bits coagulating in the dust, the crimson hand pointing an accusatory finger at man's cupidity. What was happening? No one in his family had taken much interest in what was happening in the country until then. The problems in the neighbourhood itself were enough of a headache, who had the time to bother with politics! But under the circumstances, it was no longer possible to ignore the outside world. Like thousands of other Indians like them, the women of the house were stupefied and bewildered in the face of the divisionary, separatist demands of a population that had always lived as one until then. Muslims, Hindus and Sikhs lived together in tolerance, which made it even more difficult to understand the massacres that were taking place. Even the English, who risked the alleys at night to slink discreetly into dancers' quarters, had always been welcomed courteously. Shanwaz for his part, *wanted* to understand. At ten, he was becoming aware of right and wrong. Barely out of a stagnant childhood ruined by his mother's absence, he was now confronted by monstrosities beyond his understanding.

'Divine laws have gone up in flames,' explained Pran Chowdhry, their next-door neighbour. This Hindu merchant born in the old city had never stepped out beyond the high walls built by Emperor Akbar. He liked the concentration of humanity scuttling about in the enigmatic labyrinth of its alleys, its typical Asian smells, and the harmony that reigned between Hindus and Muslims, which to him seemed unique. 'The English have decided to give us our freedom by dividing the country in two. Why this stupidity when we have lived in peace for centuries!'

Men like Pran were in no doubt that the English were largely responsible for these dramatic changes. In the former capital of the empire of *A Thousand and One Nights*, Muslim emperors had reigned for almost a thousand years without any conflict with the Hindus. But the British, with their Cartesian logic, saw Hindus and Muslims as diametrically opposite and irreconcilable beings. After colonizing India, they had followed a policy of 'divide and rule'. And it had worked better than they had thought it would. In the nineteenth century they had sowed the seeds of discord between Hindus and Sikhs, leading to clashes between the two communities. Then, in 1905, the Viceroy of India partitioned Bengal, the large eastern province, so that Muslims and Hindus could be in their own separate areas. Although the experiment was aborted six years later, it influenced millions of Muslims who felt increasingly looked down upon by Hindus. Over the years, the gulf between them had deepened everywhere you looked. It smothered and mocked all hollow efforts for reconciliation.

Pran was extremely preoccupied with reading the papers. He could sense irreversible changes approaching. But he held on to the vain hope that Lahore's old city, isolated behind its ramparts, would be spared the violence that had ravaged the region since August 1946. Demonstrations by Muslims across India had degenerated into massacres under the pretext that the Hindus and the English were refusing the partition of the country into two entities – one Muslim and the other Hindu and Sikh. The Muslims created a political party, the Muslim League, to fight for their demands and to prove that they were ready to stand alone in their fight for independence, and use force if necessary.

Gandhi, whom Pran worshipped like most Hindus for his non-violent fight against the colonizer, was deeply distressed. He had personally visited the Bengal villages where Muslims, instigated by fanatics and stories of how fellow Muslims had been exterminated in Calcutta, had killed, raped, looted and burned, and forced their Hindu neighbours to eat the meat of sacred cows. It broke the old man's heart, he who had been fighting for the past thirty years without having shed a drop of blood, to see his compatriots indulging in such savagery at a time when the country was preparing to rid itself of the British yoke. The fratricidal war had reached Punjab without really affecting Lahore.

But one March morning in 1947, hundreds of Hindus and Sikhs waving swords and sabres in the air had marched through Anarkali bazaar shouting, 'Death to Pakistan!' as they tore down Muslim League flags from the shops. Tension had mounted. Six thousand houses were burned and several hundred people were killed. Meanwhile, the papers announced the arrival of Lord Mountbatten, the last Viceroy of India, in Delhi delegated by the British monarchy to pave the way for the country's independence and its partition. Violence erupted again at its official announcement on the 3rd of June 1947. In a village not far from Lahore, ninety Hindu women jumped into a well, for fear of the Muslims, preferring to die rather than convert to the religion of the impure.

Shanwaz, whose only vivid memory related to his religion was that of his circumcision, had never seen any difference between his Hindu neighbours and his own family. Of course, they didn't get water from the same well, didn't eat the same kind of food, and never married into each other's families, but was that reason enough to pit them against each other? And now separate them? In the space of a few days, the religious fervour had doubled as much in the temples as in the mosques. At street corners people eyed each other with suspicion. No one had any friends any longer, only possible enemies. From his window, Shanwaz would spy groups of young men on the little square behind his house. They had taken to gathering there before the curfew to shout in unison: 'We will cut the Sikhs into pieces! We'll drink the blood of the Hindus. We won't leave even one of their children alive!'

Pran and his family were terrified. Shanwaz kept them company in the evenings. He had a liking for their youngest girl, a young beauty who made his heart beat uncontrollably. She was the same age as Laila and the two ravishing young girls were friends. But Naseem had now forbidden Laila from playing with Mandakini. 'Everyone is to stay in their own home,' she would say.

Shanwaz no longer listened to his mother. After being abandoned to his fate five years ago, he had taken his existence into his own hands. And he had also grown a lot. His body had become longer and firmer. He appeared older than his ten years. Only his face still had a childish grace, his mother's delicate features, immense jet-black eyes with long, naturally-curled lashes. He let a thick lock of his straight hair fall on the right side of his face, convinced that it lent him a masculine air. A way of affirming himself in this world where, if he wanted to exist, he could rely only on himself and no one else.

Pran had told him about Muhammad Ali Jinnah, a severe, unbending messiah who was terrorizing Hindus and setting himself up as the supreme leader of the Muslims. This lawyer hoped to use his oratorical skills to be as influential as Gandhi. With a condescending smile on his bony face, the severe man had lashed out, 'Either we will provoke India's division, or her destruction.' His determination had finally broken his opponents. After much hesitation, but without any choice left to them, the Hindus and the English had given in to his wishes to take over the western and eastern parts of India. These new territories would be re-named Pakistan or 'The land of the pure'. Pran was afraid. Afraid that he would be chased away to a place where he knew nothing, and no one. Afraid of being tortured, trapped in this hate that had blossomed from the cupidity of men. The transformation of the other into something that had to be destroyed before it destroyed you had become a pressing necessity.

'Of course not,' Shanwaz would reassure him, unable to visualize the possibility of such a tragedy, despite Pran's judicious explanations. He couldn't bear to think that he'd never see little Mandakini again. 'We will protect you. I promise nothing bad will happen to you. Who could possibly force you to leave your house?'

The violence, the massacres, and the crimes all intensified with every passing day that August in 1947. Revolted by the treatment meted out to them, Hindus and Sikhs started retaliating by attacking Muslim symbols and began to close in on the Badshahi neighbourhood which had been spared the conflict until then through respect for its place in Islam. Pran recounted a story to Shanwaz to illustrate the absurdity of this Partition. Hindus had thrown burning torches into a printing house that published the Quran. But the Hindu family that owned the building also lived there. Their son was trapped by the fire and died surrounded by the holy books. Outside, both Hindus and Muslims chorused their despair, trying in vain to put out the blaze.

On the dawn of the official declaration of the partition of a country and its peoples, Hindus and Muslims had the same visceral fear in the pit of their stomachs. At midnight on the 14th of August, as Shanwaz's birthday came to an end, the radios blared: 'Freedom! Freedom! We are free of white imperialism!' while the streets chanted 'Allah ho Akbar!' and 'Sat Sri Akal!', 'We don't want to be free! We want to live! Freedom is our death!' This separation desired by politicians was becoming a tragedy for all. Jinnah, Nehru and the others had naively thought that an imaginary line drawn between those who hated each other would be the answer to all problems. But they themselves were caught in the savage deluge that swept over the country. While Delhi and Karachi, the two capitals, were decorated like brides to celebrate the event, the streets of Lahore were left in ashes. And on the ashes of the thousands of dead, the city dwellers doggedly continued the genocide, dashing the hopes of those who thought that once independence came, the streets of this 'marvellous city of dreams and legends' would be paved in gold, that rivers of milk would flow within its walls. All they ever saw were rivers of blood.

Until the end of August, the inhabitants still felt very unsafe, and it made a return to normal life impossible. In the old city so many houses had been burned down that streets had become inaccessible, and there was indescribable chaos everywhere. Although the carnage had slowly stopped, Sikhs and Hindus understood that their presence was no longer desired in the heart of the 'Land of the Pure' as the 'madmen of God' called it. Pran and his kin packed their bags and said a heart-rending goodbye. For generations Shanwaz and Pran's families had maintained strong neighbourly ties. They had great respect for each other, and even though there was never any marriage between the two houses, they helped each other when the need arose, and shared an enduring affection. Shanwaz was broken-hearted. His attraction for the young

Mandakini went beyond mere friendship. She filled his dreams, and at night when he thought of her his body started to tremble and he was filled with an irrepressible desire to rub his groin against his mattress until a hot liquid spurted from his penis, but he didn't quite understand what was happening. All he could remember was the intense pleasure, and the strange vibration that went through his body, then a sensation of well-being that carried him into a deep sleep. Pran handed over the keys to his house to Naseem. Like most people who left, he was certain he would be back in a few months when things calmed down and order reigned again, and life went back to what it used to be.

But Pran Chowdhury never came back.

In September, the weather echoed the human chaos. Torrential rains brought floods and cut off all communication. Train traffic going to India slowed down and the rain brought all sorts of diseases on the poor wretches taking the path to exile on foot. The Partition threw twelve million people out on the roads, and killed one million of them.

October brought the cold north wind and a lull in the violence. But the exodus continued. Pakistanis left the nightmare of the violence for the bleak reality of pestilential refugee camps. The trains ceaselessly shuttled from one country to the other, trains of the deported, of despair, of death. Entire train-loads arrived from Amritsar, now on the other side of the Pakistani border, their ragged masses spilling into Lahore station. A sea of Muslims from India, eyes crazed and faces ravaged by the fatigue and grief of having abandoned their villages, their houses, and their belongings. They arrived with nothing to build a whole new life on. Shanwaz would see them wandering in the old city on the lookout for a little help, in search of a place to settle down.

One day Naseem was filled with pity for a family walking around with two exhausted, famished children, the mother ready to drop dead. They had fallen in a heap in the middle of the street, unable to go any further. She offered to give them shelter for a few days in Pran's house, but first she made them promise that they would leave when the owner returned. The skeletal man with the haggard face grabbed Naseem's hands and kissed them. They had been travelling on foot for days and nights, then on packed trains where people stepped on each other, tore at each other, and fought madly.

They had seen children suffocated, women thrown overboard, and men kill each other for a seat on the wooden benches. They hadn't had anything to eat or drink. Once inside the train, it was impossible to move or even get out to go to the toilets. People relieved themselves right where they sat, and as the journey continued, an unbearable stench pervaded the humid air. Mustafa and his wife Aisha were from Gujarat, the land of the Mahatma's youth. They could not fathom how this man they revered as a holy father although they weren't Hindus themselves, could have accepted that his own neighbours leave to live elsewhere, far from everything that had made up their existence for centuries only because they followed a different religion. They were deeply hurt, and grieved for their parents left behind because they were too old to leave, their bones breaking like a dead tree under the brutal beatings of the Hindus. They grieved for the women they had seen killed by their own families to avoid the dishonour of conversion, those thousands of martyrs whose heads were cut off to save the purity of their religion! They grieved for men castrated to prevent impure reproduction! Their last tears were for the consolation that Naseem and her cousins brought. For days on end, the women did all they could to help them survive.

Mustafa's two children, a girl and a boy, were called Sana and Omar. Shanwaz was moved by the joy that lit up their eyes when they understood that the journey had finally ended. The children were not any different despite the trauma they had suffered. Their heads were full of the usual ideas – they wanted to play, eat, and laugh. They became Shanwaz's new friends.

3

Less than a year after the Partition, Muhammad Ali Jinnah died of tuberculosis, without seeing his country grow. Three years later, his Prime Minister Liaquat Ali Khan was assassinated. These double disappearances were harbingers of sombre days to come. An already-unstable Pakistan was now also crumbling and beginning a slow death.

Shanwaz had just turned thirteen. Since the time he had witnessed the murderous folly of man, he had lost interest in the goings-on outside of his home.

He couldn't care less that Lahore was no longer the heart of Punjab, the happy province, India's richest and most fertile. He was only barely aware that it had been cleaved at the hands of the man responsible for drawing the line between India and Pakistan, Sir Cyril Radcliffe, and transformed into a painful puzzle of traumatic memories. Shanwaz didn't know that

Lahore was the ancient capital of the Empire in *A Thousand and One Nights*, the love of the Great Mughals. But he was troubled by the disappearance of so many of the treasures that had once adorned her. Most palaces and elegant houses of the old city had been burnt down. A half-fossilized memory of the past arose from their debris. When they were rebuilt after the fires, their inhabitants preferred cheaper and more resistant cement and concrete blocks over traditional wood. The elegance, magnificence and charm of Mughal architecture was fading into oblivion. But what those who came in after the Partition found most remarkable was how the inhabitants of this new country dressed – one of the first things the government had rushed to impose the very day after the proclamation of the Islamic Republic of Pakistan. Out with the immodest sari that showed off the velvet skin of the waist. Out with the drapes of disturbing femininity. Now both men and women wore the same traditional garment called the *shalwar kameez*. It was very loose, made up of a ballooning trouser tightened at the ankles, and covered by a long tunic that masked even the slightest curve in the body. Women added a *dupatta* to the whole, a light muslin veil which transformed them into graceful Madonnas. But Naseem was singularly averse to this inelegant garb that revealed nothing of their svelte figures, their fair skins, or their willowy thighs, and also rendered their existing wardrobe obsolete.

It cost a fortune to renew the costumes of a dancer who needed to be the epitome of every dream and fantasy every evening. The only ones rubbing their hands in glee were the shopkeepers of Anarkali bazaar. And yet, the change in the national dress soon seemed quite innocent when compared to the other rigid requirements that went hand-in-hand with the coming of Islam. Prostitution was quickly seen as absolute evil, and so declared illegal. This caused a serious stir in the neighbourhood. All that remained acceptable was dancing with a few musicians. For the rest, the courtesans had to take infinite precautions.

Shanwaz was still not going to school. His mother's new wardrobe had seen to that once again. He pursued his idle adolescent existence, destined to become one of Shahi Mohalla's many street boys. A useless pawn on the chessboard of a marginal society. The neighbourhood where his family lived had a peculiar reputation. To begin with, the streets had strange names. Hira Mandi, for instance, meant 'diamond market', 'Shahi Mohalla', the 'royal bazaar', 'Bazaar-e-husn', 'the beauty market'. These markets buzzed with insomniac clients by night and existed in a different time zone from the rest of the city during the day. Shanwaz had noticed four streets whose doors and windows never opened before the afternoon. It was surprisingly calm here while everywhere else the colourful, oppressive, compact crowds formed an active, tenacious, and fluid ribbon from the wee hours of the morning. In the end he had understood that there was a link between these streets and the women of his family who also did not open their eyes before the early afternoon. As a child, he was not allowed to go out at night. In any case, he had never felt the need to, although he had from time to time wondered about his mother's activities. He could sense instinctively that it was best to keep his distance from this world of women. They shared their little secrets, whispering confidences together and consoling each other over eventful nights whose disturbing activities filled his sleep.

With age his curiosity was no longer a blur and demanded precise answers. Deep inside him, strange changes were taking place. He wondered about his body, having remarked with a degree of amazement that his penis was growing steadily. He sat on his mattress and watched in amazement how the delicate member swelled uncontrollably when he thought intensely of Laila's slender body being washed naked in front of him by Naseem. He remembered very well when it had begun, some time before the Partition, when his first love, the ravishing Mandakini, used to appear in his dreams. He still thought about her sometimes, wondering why she and her family had never come back or even shown any sign of still being alive. Where could they be, these neighbours whose memories time effaced slowly with each passing day? He had since then shifted his affection to his new neighbour, but Sana was neither pretty nor intelligent, and Shanwaz was too used to living in the company of beautiful, seductive dancers – splendidly perfumed and made up dream dolls whom he watched leaving his home every night. He was soon distracted.

So he decided to follow them one evening. He wanted things to be clear, to know where they went, for whom they danced, how all these things took place. He slipped out behind their procession, determined to pierce the mystery surrounding their nightly escapades.

He was dumbstruck by what he saw. It was so bizarre – the four sleepy lanes behind his house were lit up as though it were *Eid*. But it wasn't *Eid*. Dusty electric lights had replaced the gas burners, and their dull glow lit up the most extraordinary sight that Shanwaz had ever set his eyes upon. From around 11 in the night, an indescribable multitude of men sauntered up hand-in-hand, all eyes for the scores of little salons open one beside the other on the street. When a client walked in, doors and windows were promptly closed. Outside, in the mauve glow of the night, girls on distant balconies appeared shrouded in mystery under lustreless lamps. The rich notes of *tablas* erupted from amidst the strange clamour of the dense crowds, accompanied by mingling voices in the streets.

His eyes wide with amazement, Shanwaz was quickly swallowed up by the crowd, but he made sure he didn't lose sight of his mother and located the building she had disappeared into. He hid, invisible in the shadows of a doorway, and watched her take her place in the shimmering room along with two musicians, one of whom, he realized to his great surprise, was their neighbour, Mustafa. He was playing the harmonium. The other was a pudgy, effeminate tabla player with scant hair pasted in lines across his bald pate and a sinister air about him. One of his aunts came to join them. She was like a shapeless mass on the floor with a minuscule table in front of her on which she prepared *paans* – sweet delicacies wrapped in betel leaves that daubed the mouth in a brilliant blood-red and made you want to spit every minute, but left your mouth fresh like the first morning of the world. She had also placed a little silver spittoon by her side, and constantly bent her head into it to eject her uninviting spittle.

They had barely settled down when a man entered. Shanwaz hadn't seen him come out of the crowd. He saw him from the back, a long, youngish silhouette in a good quality beige shalwar kameez. The welcome reserved for him suggested that this was not his first time here. Shanwaz keenly observed what went on. The aunt invited the man to sit on a mountain of silky cushions on the floor and signalled the musicians to close the door and the shutters. Shanwaz had just enough time to make out the face of the man who had hit his mother the night when as a five year-old he had rushed to help her. What was he doing here after all these years? He jumped out of his hiding place impatiently, angry that he could no longer see anything. He could only hear the musicians begin a plaintive melody which slowly gained in tempo and rhythm. Then he heard a woman's gentle, lilting voice as though she was drawing her breath from deep within herself, the deepest inhalation brought to the throat and expelled in a dull, almost bass voice which suddenly became light, volatile, then deep and sensual.

It was Naseem singing! His mother! It was the first time he was hearing the velvety richness of this suave, languorous voice that seemed to have descended from the heavens.

That night, from behind the walls of his room, he understood that his mother loved the man who had hit her.

Laila's eleventh birthday was the occasion for a grand feast. Naseem was beside herself with excitement. Cooks, musicians and tailors paraded up and down the house for days, flowers and garlands were placed on each floor by the cousins, and incense and perfumed oils were burned.

On the morning of the big day, Naseem rose at dawn for once. She had to prepare her daughter according to a precise ritual. First she had to wash her several times in running water to purify her and bring out the exquisite perfume of her young skin. Laila had sat in Naseem's room for several hours and learned about the subtleties, the difficulties and the secrets of her future career from her mother. Naseem had deprived Shanwaz of an education and left him illiterate and ignorant all these years to be better able to invest in her daughter, as her mother had done for her. In any case, what could Shanwaz complain about? He would never have to work because she would see to his needs as long as she could, and Laila would take over later. But first, Laila needed to learn that to be a dancer in Hira Mandi meant maintaining the hedonistic traditions of courtesans from the time of Mughal emperors. These resplendent, finely educated artists of immense talents had once initiated young princes to the world of women to which they had no access in their own homes. While the days of princes at Hira Mandi were long over, other men had taken their place – the haute bourgeoisie, politicians, businessmen, all looking for pleasures in their company that were not to be found elsewhere in the land of

Islam. From a tender age, Naseem had taught Laila how to smile at a man, welcome him, and make him comfortable, and to subjugate him with her beauty, seduce him with her gestures, and tame him with her intelligence and manners from the great era. Dance and singing were but the gilded facade of the fascination and pleasure.

Guests streamed in. Friends too. Neighbours. Musicians. The cousins played host and sat everyone down under the huge red shamiana that billowed in the little square behind the house. Under this big tent erected for important ceremonies, guests took their places on chairs or on cushions on the floor. They all brought gifts and flowers. They were served a variety of sumptuous dishes, meats, kebabs, pulao, and leftovers were given to the patiently cowering beggars already posted at the gates. On a stage covered in white cloth, musicians accorded their instruments. The fierce early summer heat made the already-feverish air even more electric as everyone waited for young Laila to make her appearance. She finally arrived, hidden from view by the women of the family who formed a colourful band around her. Once she was on the stage they all moved away to reveal the child metamorphosed into a woman. A murmur of amazement went through the crowd and well beyond the cloth walls.

Laila was unrecognizable, dressed like a Mughal princess in a long red silk dress tied in at the waist with a gold scarf, and a transparent gold-embroidered veil over her long hair thrown over her right shoulder. Her face was theatrically painted – red mouth, charcoal eyes –, and a gold ring adored her nose. Apart from her minuscule size, she looked twenty. Behind her the musicians launched into a pulsating rhythm. Intimidated, Laila went down on her knees, bent her head and hid behind her two hands spread out like fans before her face. Her bedroom eyes slowly looked around, both cheeky and chaste at the same time. No wavering gesture, no hesitation in the movement of the head, just a slight tremor in the nostrils – the child was already mistress of her art. She stood up, turned towards the musicians, stretched out an arm and ushered them into the first steps of her dance with a movement of her hand and the vibrations of her heavy anklet-laden feet. This was the start of what the women of Hira Mandi referred to as 'the ring-opening ceremony'. The nose-ring was a symbol of virginity, to be removed in the evening by the man who offered the most for it, to mark Laila's début in the profession.

Shanwaz had stayed away from the festivities. In fact, nobody had even bothered to include him. He had joined the procession of guests and followed the ceremony unfolding from a distance. He was overwhelmed by the beauty of this child he had watched growing up before him and was unable to think of as his sister. He was wont to imagine this graceful, sensual marvel of nature, this miniature woman who wasn't quite a woman, and whose budding breasts gave him crazy hard-ons, on someone else's bed that very evening. And yet, under the shamiana that night there was many a man ready to pay the price for the ultimate satisfaction of being the first.

While the child danced, the negotiations took place with the dancer's mother according to the custom. There was no limit to Shanwaz's shock, his bewilderment and his anger when he realized that the man who led Laila away at the end of the ceremony was the one who had hit his mother.

After that first night of savouring the magic of Hira Mandi, Shanwaz was unable to stay away. He loitered around there almost every night with his friend Omar, Mustafa's son. The two boys were of the same age and had become friends when the new neighbours moved into Pran's deserted house. For long, Omar had no idea where his father went in the evenings. He found out when Shanwaz took him along one night without telling him where they were going. Omar was far from shocked, instead he envied his father his place in such a fascinating performance. He remembered how back in India, Mustafa's only passion was playing the harmonium. Exhausted by the endless kaleidoscope of days, he would return from the fields, grab his harmonium and leave for other horizons. His eyes would close and he would be in places where nobody could follow him. The harmonium had found its place among the meagre belongings they had brought with them. Naseem was thrilled with the musician in Pran's house. She had offered him the job of one of her musicians who had undertaken the journey in the other direction to go to India. It was a godsend for him, not knowing what else he could have done there, and he was doubly grateful to this beautiful neighbour for having first given them a roof above their heads to start their lives again, and then a job. A musician! He could not have imagined even in his wildest dreams that he would one day be *only* a musician. He went to the Badshahi every day to thank Allah, his knees deep in the prayer mat as he kissed the soil of this generous land.

Omar had not inherited his father's talent. In India he used to go to school but now in Lahore nobody cared much about his education. He was an idler like Shanwaz, and didn't care for much apart from the women of Hira Mandi. The two boys would spend entire days lying on the mattress in Shanwaz's room, staring at the ceiling, exchanging vague ideas about the world their lives revolved around. They lived in a void without any perspective other than the uselessness of days going by, always the same, filled with nothing and no one. Only the rounds of the ice-cream man still kindled any sort of emotion in Shanwaz. How impatiently he used to wait for the little tootle ending in two delicious whistles that was music to his little ears. It was once the be-all and end-all of the interminable days when his life didn't extend beyond the coloured glass in the window.

In this Shanwaz was no different from the other men in his vicinity. He had only to lean out of the window to look inside other houses where they all languished from morn till night, eating and drinking on the mattresses that became the epicentres of their parasitic lives. Being a dancer's son in Shahi Mohalla was the worst fate for a boy. What could he have done in any case? What could he aspire to without even an inkling of an education? His mother fed and lodged him and gave him the few rupees he had in his pocket. Her authority over him made him so vulnerable before women that it seemed as though the city's dust had choked the cogs in his brain whenever he was confronted with any person who wasn't part of his family.

He had never stepped out of the Shahi Mohalla microcosm, never gone beyond one of the thirteen doors that marked the limits of the old Mughal city. He had no idea until then that another city existed around them out there. Not because it didn't interest him. But because he just hadn't thought about it. How could he think about something that nobody had ever spoken to him about. He was sixteen, and for sixteen years he had been breathing in air like a fish taking aimless rounds in a bowl.

He always found his way back to Shahi Mohalla and its troubled air, the women who made him lose his head, the crowds of men like moths in a panic when light suddenly shone on them, the pulsating rhythm and the sensual voices that filled the night sky. He also dreamed of entering a salon, of being welcomed with reverence, then settling into the cushions, breathing in the stale perfumed air, and letting himself be subjugated by the woman who would stand before him and bewitch him to ecstasy. But he didn't have the money to play at being the client. Nothing to assuage the desire that haunted him day in and day out. His mother's moans were becoming unbearable for him. He was lucky to be spared his sister's because she received clients on the last floor of the house. The frustration of having so many women around him and yet being alone brought out a bestiality in him that only his mattress was witness to.

Then one day, Omar gave him a solution to his money problems. He just needed to open his eyes to see what was happening in some corners of the neighbourhood. As he walked down a dark alley one night, Omar had come across a group of young boys preparing a brownish substance in a spoon which they held over a flame. Their dilated pupils confirmed his suspicions about the nature of the substance they were ingesting. One of them was an adolescent whom Omar vaguely knew.

'You want some?'

'What is it?'

'Opium.'

Why not, thought Omar, without apprehension. He sat down with them. The boy asked to be paid two rupees first, not an insignificant amount for Omar. But he acquiesced and emptied his pockets. The boy poured the contents of the spoon into a pipe and offered it to him. The first drag scorched the back of his throat leaving behind a burning bitter after-taste. He wasn't used to smoking, and his coughing made the others laugh. But he went on. He wanted to get his money's worth. He puffed at the pipe several times, disappointed by the lack of sensation, inhaling the fumes like he was advised to do by the boys. Then the effect was violent and savage. His head spun and everything became fuzzy like a thick winter fog that falls brutally from the skies. He felt the bile rise in his throat and struggled to hold it back, so he lay down, closed his eyes and waited for it to pass. And then, slowly, a feeling of well-being crept over him, growing stronger every minute, pervading his senses with a serenity he had never felt before. How long did he lie there? A minute? An eternity? He had no idea. When he told Shanwaz about his experience, he was still too groggy to find the right words to express the immense happiness he had discovered.

Shanwaz also took a liking to it. Besides, this ambrosial liquid didn't just open the doors to absolute pleasure, he also made money re-selling little sachets of opium that he was told came directly from Afghanistan, not that he even knew where that was on a map. His life underwent a profound change. His days with Omar changed completely. His world was adorned in colours which had earlier escaped his eye, and his morbid desires vanished, blown away like the dark of the day, as did the frustrations that made him scream with pain in his solitary bed. His entire being was suddenly light, and his young man's body with its tight muscles and bronze skin was ridding itself of the violence of adolescent desires. But the desire for women still raged within.

One afternoon, he left Omar in his room with his head in the clouds, and climbed to the second floor. He entered the narrow corridor that led to Laila's room and knocked gently at the door.

'Yes?'

'Can I come in?'

'Of course!'

He closed the door behind him. Laila was sitting in the middle of her bed mending one of her dresses. She was surprised by his presence. He sat down beside her, intimidated by the intimacy he had provoked by entering her room for the first time. Laila liked the colour blue as much as her mother liked pink – the curtains, the bed cover, the cushions and even the carpet were a pretty light blue. Naseem had bought her a real bed with gilded wrought iron legs. The room exuded the femininity of a mature woman, and even the perfume was too heady for this barely twelve-year old child. At this time of the day, the small, coloured, square window panes of the two bow-windows that gave onto the street filled the room in a soft yellow glow. Laila went on with her sewing but Shanwaz interrupted it to ask in a voice that opium had made deep and sensual whether she was getting used to the long nights, not daring to frankly ask her what was really on his mind. The men? Yes, what did she do with the men? How was her first night with that man he hated? Had he become one of her regulars? Had she stolen him from her mother? But he...

His hand slowly moved towards the sewing lying on her lap, picked it up and dropped it on the floor. Her eyes widened in surprise but she didn't protest. He took her by the shoulders and looked at her intensely, then very gently he pulled her towards him and placed his head on the nape of her neck. He could hear her breaths become shorter but she didn't move. Laila loved her brother, and although this enigmatic person had never given her a second glance during her childhood, she had always hoped that one day he'd take some interest in her. Now here he was, pressed against her, and the joy she felt made her oblivious to the man running his hand through her hair, down her body and then on her breast which he took in his hands with a strange tenderness. She forgot that he was her brother. Not sensing any resistance, Shanwaz brought his face down towards Laila's breasts and passionately kissed them through her clothes. She held his head and pressed it hard against herself. Shanwaz threw her on the bed and clumsily took her clothes off. His heart skipped a beat when he saw the artful velvet of her sweet almond-perfumed skin, the perfect lines and mysterious curves, so much beauty offered to him alone.

She let him revel in it and then helped him take his clothes off. When they were both finally naked, the two young bodies met with feline grace. Sensing that she was his first woman, she guided him, channelled his confusion, and spread her legs wide enough so he could find his way to the unknown, soft, narrow passage that haunted his nights. He plunged into the path that would lead him to the heart of darkness without the slightest hesitation when he understood that there was nothing else to understand and no more questions to ask.

Laila became Shanwaz's mistress. His official courtesan. In fact she became so important that there was nothing left for the others. Their afternoon games became more and more erotic. Although Shanwaz was initiated by Laila, he lost no time in learning to master their bodies. She had wanted to share his opium illuminations with him. They would take a few drags and drift off into other lands, sail the high seas of fantasy, shamelessly give in to their desires, and be carried away by the most passionate, the most perverse embraces. They took pleasure in their pleasure of the damned and at the idea of braving one of the most terrible taboos.

This went on for three years. Three years of a passionate, exclusively carnal relationship. They were Shanwaz's happiest years, happiness hidden from the rest of the world. When Laila left to dance in the evenings, he locked himself up in his room and smoked till he was no longer in his senses, to forget that from that moment on his sister was no longer his.

One night, Laila didn't come back. That evening, a pompous man of such elegance and presence entered the salon and he so impressed the musicians that they were almost unable to play. Everyone knew that this great landowner in his thirties was Nawab Muhammad Nawaz Khan, one of Punjab's last princes, an extremely rich and highly cultivated man who loved music, women and alcohol, and who continued to live in his palace like a real Mughal, surrounded by a coterie of servants, singers and musicians. Spotting Laila through the large window of the little room as he passed by, he had stopped, mesmerized by her beauty and the intelligence of the beauty which spoke of all she knew about the subtle pleasures of life. Once she had danced and sung, he offered to take her back with him. Laila could not refuse. She was going to go out of the old city's walls for the first time. She was all the more excited because she liked the man. None of her clients had managed to give her even the slightest shiver of delight. She did her job, and did it well, simulating as required to satisfy them, but nothing more. This time she was taken away like a queen to a palace that resembled something out of *A Thousand and One Nights*.

She was filled with wonder at the sight of the room in white marble with its amber drapes and its four-poster bed, and basked happily in the fascinated gaze of the gentle, considerate prince. He served her wine in a silver goblet. She had never drunk alcohol before and the little she gulped went immediately to her head. When he finally decided to make love to her, she pushed him back, laughing. He lost his balance and found himself on the floor at the foot of the bed. Laila laughed out loud and the man felt his honour was being scoffed at. He reached under his pillow, pulled out a gun and fired.

A red stain spread on the white silk sheets. Laila collapsed without a sound.

4

Shanwaz sat for hours on end in the sun on the roof-top terrace, his eyes riveted on the Badshahi, staring as though it had just appeared out of the blue. In all these years he had never noticed it. Sitting there facing their house, it was as much a part of the landscape as the garden below, the people that milled about in the streets, the electric poles, the unchanging sky whose existence would be discovered the day it decided to disappear. And the more he looked at it, the more aware he became of its beauty, the more he was moved. That glowing colour oscillating between purple and raspberry, the deepest pink splattered with immaculate white marble as the sun set. The combination of the two colours was the most magical thing about the massive Badshahi mosque that filled the entire horizon in front of his house. Perhaps that was why he'd never noticed it before. The imposing structure rose up above a prostrate Lahore, a symbol of the consummate Muslim. Once a marvellous cosmopolitan city, Lahore had now become one of loud-speakers calling believers to prayer. The one at the Badshahi towered over the entire city.

Shanwaz had started going there for evening prayers after he had seen the muezzin turning at the top of the minaret, stopping to send a long passionate cry to merciless god in the four corners of the sky. He would cross the Hazuri garden with quick, confident steps, pass in front of the recently-built mausoleum for the poet Allama Muhammad Iqbal, one of Pakistan's founding fathers, and climb the vast stairs that led to the entrance. He would leave his shoes there and walk into the gigantic courtyard surrounded by corridors, barefoot on the pink slabs still hot from the day, stopping to purify his hands and feet in the water from the fountain in the middle. He would then slip inside to face the *mihraab*, under the high domes finely sculpted with garlands of flowers. Prayer mats awaited the prayer-goers. Many came in the evening to pay homage to Allah, to the Prophet, and his saints. Knees bent, body bent, and head buried in his shoulders, Shanwaz prayed. He prayed like he had never done before. He had prayed like this since Laila's death. He prayed for her, for her soul to rest in peace. He prayed for Naseem, as devastated as he was by revulsion and pain.

It had been a year since mother and son had suffered the emptiness, the unacceptable solitude that her absence had plunged them into. A year since that last image that haunted their painful existence – Laila bundled in a white silk sheet brought home in a tonga by several policemen in the early hours of the morning. The fragile body that Naseem had washed one last time, her chest heaving as she wept loudly for her beloved child, so beautiful, so young. She couldn't breathe. Her pain became unbearable but she wouldn't let anyone else perform the religious rituals. Then, once she had been dressed by her mother in her red courtesan's dress where her blood had left dark stains, Laila was wrapped in a traditional Muslim *kaffan*, a long, stitchless shroud. Her face, turned towards the Mecca, rested in peaceful slumber on a heart-shaped cushion. Laila was buried the same day. The tonga carrying her to the cemetery was weighed down by flowers and followed by a procession of women wailing their distress, and dancers singing a poem that the musicians accompanied on their tablas. Shanwaz walked far behind, bent over like an old man.

In the days and weeks that followed, the house remained inaccessible, and the doors and windows stayed closed in the silence. Only the sounds of crying pierced the calm of the night. All the neighbours participated in the mourning. Such loss brought people together. For many nights Hira Mandi's lights were also in mourning. Nobody dared go back to work after such a tragedy. But life had to go on. They had to eat. And the music started again from where it had left off.

Nawab Muhammad Nawaz Khan had shown that he was not as great as his ancestor the emperor Jahangir, whose love-story still warmed the hearts of lovers. Jahangir knew the danger he was putting the beautiful Anarkali in when he fell hopelessly in love with her because he had no right over his father Emperor Akbar's slave and harem favourite. He was forbidden to even look at women of the harem. But their love was too much for them and one day the two love birds were imprudent enough to exchange a glance, a fatal exchange intercepted by Akbar. There was no playing around with honour at the Mughal court.

His deeply wounded pride made Akbar insensitive to his son's remorse, and he gave the order for Anarkali to be buried alive. When his father died, Jahangir had a beautiful mausoleum built over the poor girl's tomb and her body placed in a marble sarcophagus. Craftsmen engraved a poem on it where the Emperor expressed a pain that hadn't left him, 'Ah, if I could but look once more upon the face of my beloved, I would thank God until Resurrection day.'

Nawab Muhammad Nawaz Khan didn't throw as much as a flower on Laila's tomb. The ignominy of a public trail drove him to commit suicide, which was more a relief than a consolation for Hira Mandi's dancers.

Months went by. The cousins were the first to start working again, accompanied by the two betel-chewing aunts. Naseem found it very hard to don her princess outfits again to go dancing and singing. Her face had lost all its glow. What was worse, make-up only emphasized her lost features, the bluish circles under her eyes, and the wrinkles that suffering had drawn. Mustafa would come every day with his harmonium and sit by her side to help her start singing again. He was interminably patient, repeating the same melody a hundred times even though he was always interrupted by Naseem's sobs.

The first man to come on the evening that she re-joined her salon was the man who had once beaten her. His name was Jaffer. This rich businessman lived on the other side of the walls in a part of the city where inhabitants of the old city never went. Despite the violence of their relationship, he had become so attached to the dancer that he had accepted her demand for the ring-opening ceremony. She had not wanted a stranger for this delicate initiation. Unlike other dancers who would have been happy to give their daughter to the highest bidder, Naseem had not seen it only from the point of view of money. She had wanted her daughter to be treated well, without any of the brutality with which some men acted, monsters who had a field day, and left behind little girls tainted for life who would never be able to take the slightest pleasure in the act again.

Jaffer was a good-looking man in his forties. Coming from a family of repute, his skin was a warm brown like the colour of the very strong tea that was drunk in these parts. He was married according to tradition, to a woman that his family had chosen for him, and whom he didn't love. Of course, this had not stopped him from fulfilling his conjugal obligations of giving her three children with whom he didn't spend much time. His cloth business took up all his time. And in the evenings after a long tiresome day, he would leave the austere family ambiance for some amusement in Hira Mandi. Naseem had always been his favourite dancer. It gave him intense pleasure to see her mature. When her body moved under her silky clothes, a violent desire overwhelmed him, and when he finally found himself against her it made him so rough that he sometimes ended up hurting her. She would then insult him, which he couldn't stand. Which is what had happened the night Shanwaz had clung onto his trousers. He had lost his cool, and was filled with shame and great frustration. Not quite himself, he had left the house shouting profanities he had later regretted.

After the tragedy of Laila's death, he had been unable to approach Naseem. He was overcome by distress. He remembered Laila from that night – the only one – spent with a child the same age as his own daughter. He had been deeply troubled by it, not knowing what to do to stop from hurting her. She had been incredibly agile, taking the lead when she saw that he was ill at ease. She had stripped him, then taken off her red silk dress, had lain down beside him to gently caress, kiss and excite him. Was it Naseem who had taught her all these gestures that she executed with perfect command, without the slightest emotion, or trembling shyness? She had pulled him to her, taken his immense, hard penis and introduced it into her soft, minuscule slit. He had entered without pushing, without violence, until he could feel the delicate resistance which he was supposed to break and cross. Which he did. He heard a long sigh but he couldn't tell whether it was out of pain or pleasure. Blood ran between their thighs. Laila's head was buried in his shoulder, her long hair spread all over the pillow. He didn't dare move. Then she went wild, pulling his big, strong penis into herself until he came. That child was made for love. She had no limits. She would drive any man who came between her legs crazy.

Naseem was touched by Jaffer's presence that evening. Would she have been able to dance for a stranger? She wasn't sure. For Jaffer, yes. His eyes gave her strength. She remembered to use the gestures he liked, and sang a long text by the poet Faiz who was already rotting in the jails of the brand new Islamic republic of the 'Pure' where the beautiful Almaz, one of Hira Mandi's most famous courtesans, took gifts for him. Jaffer was gentle with Naseem that night. Her first night of love since Laila had left. He entered her gently, sensing how much she needed to wrench her heart out of the suffering that was burning up her life and consuming it.

It would have been easy for him to take refuge in opium. But Shanwaz preferred religion, which seemed like a strange choice to Omar who continued to take and sell drugs. It was so easy in this neighbourhood littered with drug addicts. Miserable wretches who died alone on the pavements, a sight that now disgusted Shanwaz. Death distressed him. There was too much suffering in it. His withdrawal had inflicted slow agony on him. His body trembled, he broke into cold sweats, and his head spun from giddy spells and uneasiness, like an infernal spiral full of nightmares. He felt as though he was asleep standing up in a strange slumber. Everything moved slowly. Noises encircled him like huge arms closing in to suffocate him. But he held on. And progressively, the need left him. His spirit recovered a lucidity that made him look squarely at Allah. From then on, he was no longer alone.

Religion had been absent all of his childhood; his circumcision was the only concession made by his mother. For the rest, he was hardly told anything about the Quran, a little about the Prophet and, when it was necessary, about Allah. His curiosity had been aroused during the Partition, when the world exploded in convulsions of horror and destructive fury. What did they mean, all these deaths in the name of a God that all declared was theirs? What difference could there be between that of the Hindus and that of the Muslims? The question had disturbed him. Until now, he had listened halfheartedly to the muezzins in normal times and felt oppressed during Ramadan when the imams crying out their prayers all through the night, refused to allow anyone in the neighbourhood even a moment's sleep. He had learned a lot since then. The Hindus had been chased away for their adulation of a multitude of bizarre divinities whereas Muslims had a single God, Allah – the only God worthy of veneration. Yet, he found out that even within his own religion there existed factions, conflicts, hate. Quite obviously, man could never agree on the same things. He was Shi'a like the entire old city, but the rest of the country was Sunni. Where did the difference lie? He had been told that at Karbala in Iraq, the Sunnis had killed the grandson of the Prophet and the son of Ali, imam Hussein, because they did not see him as Muhammad's rightful successor. The imam and some of his followers had been ambushed and then brutally murdered by the bands of Yazid the usurper. No one was spared, not even the children. Hussein was beheaded and his sister Zainab dragged to the palace where Yazid was playing with her brother's head. Far from falling into despair, she had taken up the struggle with other followers. Their descendants never forgot the incident in Karbala and it became the holy city of the Shi'as.

Shanwaz had reacted with pride, seeing himself as Ali's heir, fighting with the assassins of the Prophet's descendants. He had a mission. To accept his religion, his origins. To pray.

But he didn't know how to read or write. Being illiterate at almost twenty was a daily handicap which cut him off not only from his religion because he could not read the Quran, but also from the rest of the world. The rare newspapers around were inaccessible to him. It was time to jump out of the little goldfish bowl he had been living in. He was disgusted by the apathy that had made him so lazy. His idea of society was incredibly uniform. Without any depth. Always the same streets, the same façades, the same people, the same stories. A little fresh air would do him good. He couldn't face himself in the mirror. Shame crept up into his sunken cheeks. None of the feminine roundness, which had once given his adolescent face an air of serene beauty, remained. The time for candid happiness was over. Laila had taken everything with her to her tomb. He had thought life was impossible without her, and had been prepared to join her if he hadn't understood that such an act would have killed Naseem. No more tragedies! The neighbourhood had had its fair share of those. Women were battered, mistreated and abandoned every day. That deceitful Jinnah, proclaiming loud and clear that in coming to Pakistan and leaving discrimination and contempt behind in India, Muslims would be free and respected. Yet what had these women seen but the same discrimination, the same contempt, but this time in the sacred name of Islam which went even further to proclaim prostitution as the worst damnation?

The police came to Shahi Mohalla one day, and took over a house to convert it into a police check post. This heralded bleak days for the courtesans. Corrupt to the bone, these representatives of the state negotiated their leniency at a high price. So nothing ever changed, thought Shanwaz. How was the world to change? It would mean being the change. And not waiting for everything to fall into his mouth like the bread balls he threw at the pigeons that had overridden Lahore's roofs. But how was he to extricate himself from this haven of drugs and prostitution? None of the people he knew could help him, they were stuck in the same quagmire as him, living off their mothers, sisters, aunts and cousins, like rats in a sewer.

Shanwaz imagined that real life existed somewhere outside these walls, outside the fiery old ramparts coloured by the rays that washed the city red every evening, as though its bricks held the blood of all the suns it had seen dying. One day, he leapt onto a tonga and headed for the new city, determined to find a job while he learned to read and write. Anything that would give him a few rupees a day so he could find himself a teacher and get an education.

On exiting the old city through Lahori Gate, the tonga took a wide open avenue lined with splendid buildings in a style that didn't resemble the architecture of his neighbourhood at all, in the same breathtaking pink as the Badshahi. His eyes widened with wonder like a child's before a magician. Every avenue he crossed had its own display of extraordinary palaces, each better than the other, in the middle of vast green parks, majestic trees and lawns as silky as prayer mats. These were the sumptuous villas where Muslims, Sikhs, Hindus, Christians, and Parsis had lived without discrimination, their extravagantly dressed women dancing into the night to the rhythm of tangos. How could he ever have imagined these niches of pure delight in these vast celestial gardens? His eyes knew but broken bricks, old stones, worm-eaten wood, grey cement, repulsive gutters, nauseating smells, and the heavy, squalid atmosphere of a decomposing city.

Ah, this city! The air seemed pure here, so lovely to breathe in! Only harmony and beauty reigned here. Even passers-by looked different, nimble-footed, their heads held high, as though they had been delivered of all the weight of the alleys that pitilessly crushed the inhabitants of the Mughal city. Shanwaz, the survivor of a dirty, dilapidated world, discovered the Eden promised by Muhammad Ali Jinnah. 'The Land of the Pure!' The obvious demonstration of Islam's superiority over the world. He had never seen so many well-bred people in such a short space of time, with their open faces and provocative eyes. They crossed the civil lines, the city once built for the English, where no Indians were allowed, and where there were no open drains, no dirt and excreta anywhere, and then finally they reached the first constructions of the modern city where the foundations of an upright and educated society were being laid.

He jumped off the tonga nimbly, full of hope. This was where his new life would begin. He was certain of it. Why hadn't he thought of it earlier? He would surely find work in this idyllic society full of *joie de vivre,* and welcoming, understanding inhabitants. He started walking down a wide tree-lined street full of shops. Even the heat was milder and more bearable here. He walked for long, attentively watching the activities and the rhythm of the shop owners, intimidated, and unsure of how to ask for work. But these people looked so nice. He would excuse himself for his lack of education.

The first shop keeper he spoke to was a tall, imposing man in an immaculate white shalwar kameez, who scrutinized him from head to toe.

'Sir,' started Shanwaz, 'please, I would like to work.'

The man seemed to be looking over his head, and Shanwaz instinctively turned around, thinking he was being shown something. But he didn't see anything in particular. When he turned back, the man had gone back into the shop and was attending to his business. Shanwaz approached him again.

'Sir, I need a job. Would you have something for me?'

He thought he saw exasperation written in the man's eyes. The man shooed him away with a wave of his hand, without a word, like a miserable beggar. How could he get out of the situation without losing face? thought Shanwaz, unable to believe how he had just been treated. He finally went off as though nothing had happened, convinced that he had chanced upon the only boor in this beautiful city of Islam.

At the end of the day, he could no longer keep count of the boors. All had, without exception, rejected him, but he couldn't understand why because nobody even spoke to him. Perhaps he didn't speak their language? Shanwaz learned later that with their accents, the progeny of Shahi Mohalla distinguished themselves as easily as being branded on the forehead with an iron. In Pakistan, being a prostitute's son had the same stigma as being an untouchable in India. Impossible to shake off. No one would ever escape Shahi Mohalla ghetto. His return to the walled neighbourhood was less glorious. His despair at going back home had reached such heights that he had just one desire, to find Omar and his junkies and end up on a pavement somewhere.

But instead he went to the Badshahi for the evening prayers.

He had grown up amidst the odours of women and the stink of semen, but he decided that the time had now come to purify himself. This year he would participate in the Shi'a *Ashura* pilgrimage commemorating the massacre of the Prophet's grandson, imam Hussein. As the new moon appeared, an imam announced the start of *Muharram*, a month of mourning for the martyr, thirty days during which laughter and pleasure were formally prohibited, and were punishable offences. Multitudes of black flags fluttered over Shi'a mosques and homes. Children distributed fresh water in the streets, in memory of the terrible thirst that Hussein and his followers had suffered in the desert. Shanwaz stood in the middle of the wailing crowd, and intently listened to the imam recreating Hussein's tragedy by reaffirming the exemplary role of the Karbala martyrs who had risen up against tyranny and oppression. On the first night, grinders everywhere sharpened knives and sabres.

From the crack of dawn, Shanwaz followed the procession through the old city, amidst the pilgrims violently flagellating their bare backs with knives attached to a cord. The more inspired cut their faces and torsos with sabres. Shanwaz almost fainted with pain at the first blow to his shoulder. He tottered. But not wanting to lose face before the tearful, puffy-eyed women and the hysterical screaming men all crying for his pain, he pulled himself up, gathered all his energy and continued to flog himself until the ecstasy wiped out the violent burning sensation. There was blood everywhere. It flowed from his back, on his arms, his hands. His ecstatic eyes lit up the diabolical features of his red face, which had become like everybody else's. Dervishes with long hair and crazed bloodshot eyes shouted slogans against the Sunnis, then suddenly shut up and chanted psalms and slurred litanies about blood, vengeance and martyrdom. A delirious mob followed the bloodied procession that surrounded Ali's white horse majestically draped in a green and gold mat. The tormented animal was finding it difficult to keep its calm. It was excited by the smell of blood and it seemed to share in the ecstasy of the men around it. It was frothing at the mouth, and its jerky walk made it seem like a broken puppet. This went on for thirty days and thirty nights to the sound of a dull noise like a gigantic heart beating in the background. The crying inhabitants brought water and food to the bloodied pilgrims who looked like zombies from hell.

When Shanwaz finally returned home, he could barely stand; his clothes were in tatters and stuck inside the deep gashes on his back. He stopped at his aunts' place to pay them the respect of a pilgrim back from a crusade against Evil. A long red sliver of betel juice chinked into the old copper spittoon with absolute precision. They stared at him, not any more moved by his pitiful state than by his mystical words. He didn't insist.

Once in his room, Naseem took care of him like she used to when he was a child, with a wet cloth on his wounds, her tender motherly gaze on her little one in pain. She had always been quite far-removed from religious things, but was fiercely proud of this son who was close to the Prophet and his saints.

Shanwaz definitively abandoned Allah's sacred path the day he read in the Quran that eternal life by the Prophet's side awaited 'believers' and the 'pure'. His days were so full of boredom and went by so slowly that he was petrified at the idea of an existence sans end punctuated by bloody pilgrimages, and he swiftly renounced the path to eternity. Islam then seemed to him like something from the end of time.

Shanwaz and Naseem spoke little to each other. He had not confided in his mother for years. The last moments of tenderness harked back to a time he had naively believed himself to be the apple of her eye. Although she had been involved in her womanly world, constantly preyed upon by problems, his passion for Laila and their sensual afternoons had not gone unnoticed by her. Despite the horror and shock she had felt on discovering her children's incestuous relationship, she hadn't been able to end what she thought of as inevitable and incurable. Her daughter's death had plunged her into mourning, and had brought her closer to her son. But he had moved away, looking for an outlet for his despair. It was then that she had understood his desire to escape his position as an offspring of Hira Mandi.

'My poor child, you were born here, you will die here, and between that your life will be lived out right here.'

The words sliced through him like a knife. A terrible, unbearable prophecy. And to anchor him well and good in this world that he could not just walk out of, Naseem decided it was time to marry off her son.

5

A gust of wind picked up the dust and covered the April sun in an opaque veil. It was becoming hotter. Day by day and hour upon hour the temperature rose towards its summer intensity. No one and nothing could control this lethargy that imposed itself on everything for six months. That day in April 1953 looked like it was going to be hot but the north wind brought respite and the air became breathable, if only for a moment. Long before the sun rose, a long procession of humans resembling the 1947 exodus took the road to Pakistan, sitting on overloaded tongas, or on old rickety buses overflowing with passengers – they were everywhere, on the running boards, precariously dangling from the metal bars, on the roof, heads and arms sticking out of windows without panes. But this time they were all light-hearted and full of optimism. At the border crossing, the guards who were usually so uncompromising in their dictum 'each to his own country', opened the gates wide with angelic smiles, welcoming their Sikh and Hindu neighbours authorized to come across and watch a hockey final.

Of the thousands of Indians who crossed the border that day, most didn't give a toss about the match. For them, the historic meeting would be about finding a relative, a friend, a street, a house, a memory, a remnant, traces of a still-painful, recent past. When the winding tide of tongas reached the doors of the old city, the travellers spilled out into the streets and alleys, and Lahoris came out of their houses to throw their arms around them with a spontaneity that showed how much the thousands of years they had spent together in peace and friendship were still alive in them. There was much uninhibited hugging and kissing. The Sikhs and Hindus were invited everywhere that day, and the visitors didn't spend even a rupee. Doors were opened and festive dishes and litres of tea were prepared. The inhabitants always remembered the exuberance of that day.

Naseem and Shanwaz waited all day in the hope of seeing their neighbours Pran Chowdhry and his family. They asked people who went by but nobody seemed to know them. They probably didn't live in Amritsar, or they would most certainly have come. Then along came a man whom they had known well, a former shopkeeper from the neighbourhood. Once he had warmly greeted them, the man recounted the terrible odyssey of the death trains. He explained how far the Muslims and Hindus had gone in their deadly fury. When a train full of Muslims left Amritsar for Lahore, the convoy was stopped at the border by groups of Hindus who climbed on board and killed all circumcised men. In the other direction, Muslims killed those who were not. It was in one of these macabre trains that Pran was killed. His head was cut off with a blow from a sword while his wife looked on. She had fallen in the midst of the dismembered cadavers trying to protect her children. The survivors' screams of terror rent the air. Once the assassins had left, men pretending to be rescue workers had climbed into the carriages filled with the overpowering smell of blood and excreta. Seemingly intoxicated by the pestilential stink, they had killed all those who were still breathing. The man who witnessed all this owed his life to the toilet door behind which he had hidden where, miraculously, nobody had bothered to look. After hearing this terrible account, Shanwaz and his mother left in tears and waited for the streets to empty of the now-unwelcome travellers.

They all left when night fell. The procession departed in the other direction. The light-heartedness had gone, like a candle snuffed out in the remains of its own wax. A deathly silence took the procession back to the border. Even the guards had lost their smiles. The gates closed for many long years to come.

Shanwaz had been wondering for months why Naseem was hell-bent on pushing him into the tragic sanctuary of marriage. He had revolted, then moaned like the dying when she had revealed the name of the one she had chosen. No! No way! He had screamed, fighting against his unrelenting mother, whose authority he had to bow to as a son whose only right was to obey. He was petrified. No one had replaced Laila in his heart or even in his body. And now he was filled with horror at the thought of the one who was soon to fill the conjugal bed. He shivered nervously with fever, played the tragic actor, stretching his arms out towards his mother, accusing her of wanting him dead. But there was no more joking with death in the house. And he got a resounding slap across the face instead. Piqued, he left to go to the mosque for the solace that he couldn't find in his own house. And he prayed, and prayed.

On his way back, he stopped by Mustafa's house to watch the young Sana from a distance, still as unattractive, with hair that fell like rags on her sagging shoulders, waxy skin, big spherical breasts like melons, and a smile that turned into a wince as soon as she caught sight of him. Her silence was so oppressive, he wondered if she could even talk. This was the woman chosen for him, this shapeless lump, this face that lacked even a hint of light and intelligence. Distraught, he crumpled into a heap onto his mattress. He still had such big dreams in his heart. He had not given up on becoming an educated man and earning a living by himself. But he already needed such colossal stamina to fight against the social machinations of Muhammad Ali Jinnah's society, where would he find the strength to take care of that spineless, stupid being every day? He looked in every direction, but there would be no escaping it, like his status of a son of a whore, of a child of Hira Mandi, of an untouchable.

The wedding preparations took months. The two families had to agree on the young woman's dowry. Mustafa was poor. The job of a Hira Mandi musician was not much more enviable than that of a sweeper or a rag picker. There was no respect for the artist and he earned a pittance. In the Land of the Pure, he wasn't worth much more than a good-for-nothing. But Naseem didn't give in on any point. As the mistress of the house, she manoeuvred cleverly when it came to her interests. Because it all boiled down to her best interests – she wanted to marry off her son so he could give her a daughter. Who else would take care of her in her old age? She didn't for one instant believe that Shanwaz was capable of anything but losing himself in his dreams, or in some mosque visiting Allah five times a day. It was out of the question to marry him off to a dancer already sullied by the hands of the men she knew only too well. Like all mothers, she wanted a young virgin for him, a rare commodity in the neighbourhood. Mustafa's daughter would do, even though her father was poor. And so what if she didn't please Shanwaz? He had all the freedom to amuse himself with the dancers. Since when was wedlock anything but a question of interests between two families? Since when did feelings come into it? Nobody married for love. And what love could he talk about? What meaning did the word have in a society reduced to fighting for mere survival? Even in the films that had begun to show at the City Cinema at the end of the road where Naseem had her salon, reason always overcame love, with its share of tragedies and tears echoed in the faces coming out of the evening show.

The wedding took place on a beautiful, cool winter's day. A few stationary clouds hung like big fluffy meringue flowers in the navy blue space above. In the little square behind the house, the red and gold shamiana was erected once again. The bride had disappeared behind an avalanche of veils, and gold shone wherever there was a hint of skin to be seen. Outrageous make-up accentuated the irreparable damage caused by nature's absent-mindedness. Shanwaz sat in a large seat beside his wife in an outfit he found ridiculous – he was dressed all in white like a maharaja, with a voluminous turban on his head topped with a fan. The lazy audience came and went and stared at the newly-weds perched on the stage, both straight-faced and numb before this idle, silent, and listless sea of guests waiting in complete boredom for the delayed meal to be served.

After the torment of the festivities came the ominous torture of the sexual act. Shanwaz shivered with dread and the fever that flushed his body at every new challenge. Laila's silence resounded within his being, an echo of her distant disappearance. He had never touched a woman since then, so possessed was he with the demoniac force of their love. Laila, help me, he cried inwardly as he mounted the steps behind a stumbling Sana entangled in her veils and trousers.

In the room, he hardly dared glance at the pathetic sight of the poor girl, her make-up melted like butter in the sun, running in unattractive brown lines across her face, her silhouette squeezed into a shapeless, un-ironed shalwar kameez, and eyes that darted with fright whenever she dared to look up from the floor to try and understand what was going to happen next. Luckily, the feeble lamp in a corner of the room blurred the details of the pathetic spectacle they made in the night. Shanwaz finally took his courage in both hands, breathed in deeply and moved towards his wife. In deathly silence, he began the slow and fastidious undressing of the bride, as though he were plucking a daisy. She was stiff as a stick. Frightened by the huge globes hanging from her chest, and especially by her lower stomach, which he preferred not to think about, Shanwaz only removed the essentials. He did the same for himself, and once they were both lying down, began to wonder how to enter her. His penis was limp as after a cold shower. He closed his eyes and thought intensely about Laila, the magic of her body, her warm thighs that knew how to open when he was almost fainting, her tiny breasts whose pink tips pointed to the sky as soon as his tongue went over them. The efficiency of his memories surprised him. Without losing a minute he turned towards the wide-eyed Sana who was ready for a journey into hell; removed the cloth that remained between her legs, caught his penis in his hand and pushed it into the dry hole whose strange resistance he was unaccustomed to. Sana let out little cries like an animal in pain. A hot liquid flowed between her thighs and the wetness excited Shanwaz. He took her with uncontrolled lust, pushing his penis further and further into her without heeding the compulsive sobs of the young girl under him.

The couple were put on the last floor of the house. That was the place for a legitimate wife who did not belong to the profession. Two of the four cousins had left dancing to begin their households a few streets away. They came by from time to time to visit their mother and recount their sorry tales of ill-treatment, abandoned by the men they had left the profession for, now fat with repeated pregnancies. Shanwaz, who had known them in their prime, now saw them as pale reflections of the chirpy birds he had known, trembling under the weight of their charm and their grace. Their thicker waists, their grey skins, their dull hair were all signs of a broken balance like the appearance of invisible cracks in a wall covered in wallpaper.

Naseem, who was gradually reaching her fortieth birthday, knew that she would soon have to leave her salon and stop dancing. Men only wanted pubescent girls with magical youth. For a dancer, growing old meant entering the ghetto of other retired magicians, a desolate world of regrets and bitterness. Shanwaz was scared for his mother. Scared of the abyss the two aunts had fallen into, so old now that their teeth had fallen off, the hair on the tops of their heads forming a mat of grey in shreds and their bent bodies already smelling of rot. These bodies they had sold without restraint until the frame that held all the pieces together were utterly and completely worn out, dismembered like survivors of a pathetic shipwreck. They were slowly going out like two wizened candles in an old candle stand.

After his marriage, Shanwaz spent most of his time outdoors. And in the evenings, he would manage to get home as late as possible like most married men who had nothing to say to their wives, nothing to share with them, not even a tender moment in bed. When he pushed open the door to their room, nothing relieved him more than the sight of Sana sleeping. He would then be overcome with sympathy for this woman to whom he did not need to pay the sort of attention he should have. He would fall asleep at peace, wake up early the next morning and leave the house before she woke up.

He would find himself in the cool street where the only morning activity consisted of rag pickers squatting on the pavement, collecting rubbish with two wooden planks which also served as shovels to throw it all into a little mule-drawn cart. He would leave on foot, cross the garden in front of the Badshahi and reach the Roshnai Darwaza, the Door of Lights, one of the thirteen entrances to the old city. On the other side, the Ravi flowed peacefully on, lined with trees full of noisy birds. Shanwaz was deeply moved by the surreal atmosphere of the landscape in the pale pink light of the morning sun. He studied its constantly changing colours, paling under a cloud and then moving into a deeper hue. He contemplated this immaculate nature as he walked, and felt a fire rise within him, a desire to be the creator of such a work of beauty. To become a magician of colours! He thought about it. Now that he had a job, anything was possible.

Yes, he was finally working. Of the many changes of the past months, this was the most spectacular, the most inspiring. He owed it to Jaffer, the man he had so vehemently hated as a child. But the man had reached out to him one night as they passed each other on the stairs. And they had exchanged words for the first time. Jaffer knew how much Shanwaz wanted to earn a living, and had told him to come to his cloth factory. He had gone the very next day.

His life had changed since then. He had become a new man, he was now unexpectedly looking at a future before him. When he returned home in the late afternoons, he would visit Mr Brohi, a retired professor who taught him Urdu for a few rupees, apprising him of the incongruity of this language imposed on them by Muhammad Ali Jinnah when the entire city spoke Punjabi. Yet over the centuries, Urdu, the language of the Mughal courts had become the language of the Muslim community. Resembling Sanskrit and appreciated by the elite, it also had a strong emotional bond with the Quran. But Pakistani tribes had already rejected it, preferring like the Punjabis, to continue speaking their ancestral dialects. This refusal had infuriated Jinnah who insisted that Pakistan's national tongue would be Urdu and nothing else. People got all worked up. Student demonstrations were crushed with violence. Despite all this, Mr Brohi admitted that Urdu was necessary for his young student's future. Shanwaz had applied himself so diligently that his progress was surprising. Very soon he was able to read and write.

Fascinated by the young man, and sensing his immense curiosity, and real talent for art and culture, the old man didn't just teach him a language; he wanted to show him the world as he saw it through a multicoloured kaleidoscope that lent its magical hues to every moment of life. For him, every ray of sunlight was filled with divine light. He had his own way of expressing things, this professor who had already gone over to the other side where mere mortals did not always venture. Or if they did, it was with difficulty. He had reached a place where everything was radiance and ignorance. Yet his knowledge seemed universal.

'In the Tharparkar desert, strange things happen,' he liked to repeat. The population there lived in harmony with scorpions, snakes and insects. Do you know why? Because the inhabitants of Tharparkar have never killed scorpions or snakes or insects. The animals know it. And they respect them for it.'

A wide-eyed Shanwaz took it all in. Mr Brohi was a poet with a bright and generous soul. He would take flight, and all who listened to him flew with him. His little library was as important for Pakistan as the *Flor della Mar* was for Portugal. Mr Brohi's books were full of esoteric stories. Comfortably ensconced in his minuscule living room that came alive only when a guest arrived, he would share his train of thought with

Shanwaz for hours on end. Mr Brohi was proud to welcome him in his infinitely plain and remarkably clean apartment that overlooked Delhi Gate. He lived there alone with an old servant, his wife had died a long time ago and his children had left home.

Although he was profoundly Muslim, Mr Brohi advocated the idea of a state separated from Quranic law. Some years ago, he had written an article in one of Pakistan's largest circulated papers, *Dawn*, causing a minor scandal. In it he had explained that no Quranic verse could establish a state or define constitutional law. Since then, Mr Brohi, who was never to be disturbed during his five hours of daily prayers, had never gotten mixed up in politics again. He got up at dawn, and started his day with two hours with Allah before sitting down at his small desk to work at his esoteric research. Over sixty, and always impeccably attired in a crisply ironed shalwar kameez, he would receive Shanwaz by starting the lesson with a long metaphysical and religious preamble that infused him with dizzying vigour and sometimes left him on the verge of tears. For Shanwaz, who sometimes found it difficult to follow his professor's fanciful flights although he could guess at their significance, this man was a saint. He saw in him a miraculous being endowed with a third eye on the forehead, the essential eye, the eye that saw through the Being and beyond.

His contact with such a man made him grow up. It instilled immense pride in him which effaced the painful feeling of not belonging to the world. He had just begun to see light at the end of a long, infinitely long tunnel, when another mishap occurred.

As he returned one night, and barely started up the stairs, he heard his mother's voice. Her screams made the blood rush to his head. He violently pushed open the door and found himself face to face with something he had already seen – a man hitting Naseem. A stranger having a field day. Shanwaz grabbed him, pulled him away from the bed and punched him in the face. The man staggered, but he was young and strong and not giving up easily. He pounced on Shanwaz. The two men fought savagely for several interminable minutes until Shanwaz finally got the upper hand. The man left, with his face bloodied, swearing he would go to the police. Which he did.

And Shanwaz found himself in a Lahore jail. That day, he swore to get his mother out of the trade.

He spent a year in hell. One whole year of going back and forth over his short existence, of rubbing elbows everyday with aggressive men packed in cells with no space to breathe, no mats to sleep on, no water to wash with, and an unbearable stench hanging in the humid air.

Sana was an exemplary wife, neither tearful nor whimpering, and she came to see him every week with books and newspapers given by Mr Brohi, knowing that nothing would give him more pleasure. Despite the cramped space, he always found a corner to curl up and continue learning the language, and keep up with the country's current events at the same time. There was nothing inspiring in the newspapers he carefully scoured, the same tensions with East Pakistan, part of former Bengal, which was clamouring for its independence. The Muslim League, created in 1906 and which eventually became Jinnah's party, had been dealt a bitter defeat by the opposition in the last elections in 1954. The government was yet to get over this defeat. Problems were sparking off everywhere like Bengal flares. Ten years after the Partition, Pakistan was walking a tight rope between two abysses. No one had the authority or the charisma to take the country forward.

One day, Shanwaz was surprised by how Sana looked. He found her paler than usual and despite the enormous shalwar kameez under which she buried her body, he could discern a certain roundness. He mentioned it to her and saw the colour rise in her plump cheeks. She was flustered, lowered her eyes and in a barely audible voice mumbled that she was pregnant. Shanwaz was stunned.

He thought about it night and day. Being a father? He had never even dreamed about it. Even when Naseem had confessed why she wanted to get him married, it had been a blur, a woman's dream he had nothing to do with. So much had happened to him in the past year that he was completely at a loss at the thought of the arrival of a child, of his child. What was important was that it should be a girl, so Naseem could be happy.

When he came back, the little one was already four months old. She was called Aisha after her maternal grandmother who had recently died of a bad infection. Shanwaz gazed at the child and recognized Laila's face in her faint features. The shock rushed through his veins with such heat that he almost retched. The only other time he had come close to a baby, he had been five, and he remembered perfectly well the swell in his heart when his aunts and cousins had introduced him to his sister. Now, at twenty-one, in an incredible coincidence, the one that was being held out to him looked just like Laila.

Shanwaz picked up his life again but not exactly where he had left it a year ago. His professor, Mr Brohi, was dead. He was devastated. His grief reflected the attachment he felt for him. He regretted not ever having had the opportunity to express his infinite gratitude to the man who had taught him that life, no matter where it comes from, was never something to be ashamed of. He lost Mr Brohi's poetic world, but found consolation in Jaffer at the cloth factory, in his work and in the friendship of this man who could have been his father. How was one to know? The children of Hira Mandi did not have fathers. No roots to draw up the sap to build their lives on solid foundations. Nothing but lame ducks wearing away their bottoms on dirty pavements, inherent laziness instilled in their genes even before they set foot on earth. When Shanwaz looked at Jaffer, his stomach knotted, something that had happened to him quite unexpectedly one day. He had looked at this man with his pleasant physique and his open face, and suddenly felt as though he was looking at himself. But he had rejected the idea. Above all, he told himself, it was their friendship which was important. Jaffer was a man he could count on, a rare enough thing in his entourage for him to see their bond as sacred.

His days in prison had not all been negative. Amongst the rabble he had also met political prisoners. Highly educated men who had opened his eyes to the workings of the society in the other world behind the wall of shame. Some months ago, Ayub Khan, an army general, had taken over power after martial law was imposed. The general had quickly moved to prohibit all political parties and had thrown all opponents of his regime into prison. Many of them shared Shanwaz's cell for having stood up against this law that gave all the power to the army and engulfed the country in a terrible dictatorship. Although he was light years away from gleaning any of the complexity of politics, not any more than he was capable of understanding the purpose behind the sophisticated rules intended to govern the behaviour of the country's elites, Shanwaz had got the gist of things – he needed to speak English, the only key to opening the doors to proper Pakistani society. Since then he was dogged by the idea, just as a desire to paint also rose from within the depths of his subconscious. Jaffer found him a school where he went every day after work. He found English easy after Urdu, although the pronunciation sounded weird in his ears which were sharp at picking up intonations and musicality in words. He simply regretted that he had nobody to speak with as soon as he reached Shahi Mohalla.

Since Aisha's birth, Naseem had seen ghosts reappear from the past and taunt her. Shanwaz had fulfilled his promise by giving her a daughter but her striking resemblance to Laila disturbed Naseem. She saw a prophecy in the child's innocence – a reincarnation of her daughter. Why had destiny prepared this twin who stirred strange torment in her and transformed the joy of looking at the little one into a suffering? Shanwaz too was caught in the spell. Whenever the child looked at him, he saw the diabolical glint of Laila's eyes coming at him from the other world. He was so overwhelmed by it that he broke all contact with his daughter. He would get up at dawn and return when the house was asleep. Months went by. His English was getting better, but he still wasn't earning enough to support the entire family. Naseem had given up dancing, closed her salon and sent away the musicians. As the months went by she saw her clients dwindling. Even Jaffer. Ever since he had employed Shanwaz, he only made rare appearances. In her forties now, Naseem went through moments of sheer dejection. Locked up in her room, repainted candy pink to give it a dash of cheerfulness, she looked at herself in the mirror that no longer reflected the lines of her youthful beauty. The pallid glow from the neon tube lent an unbearable brownish pallor to her skin. The contours of her face were no longer as clear, she could see a slight sluggishness, yes, that was it, that progressive sluggishness that first gave women a slightly tired look, then the terrible sense of having irrevocably lost their youth.

Even her body, which she took such good care of, and had always been so proud of, was betraying her, her stomach was now rounded, thick, chubby, and her hips were enveloped in a few centimetres of fat. It wasn't because she wasn't careful – she ate just enough to survive, but nothing helped. Age … every dancer's tragedy! Age and solitude. These two torments of ageing so haunted Naseem that she lost the desire to live.

Shanwaz found her one morning, lifeless, bathed in her own blood. She had cut open her veins, a common ritual with neighbourhood prostitutes. She needed a doctor, quickly. But there were no doctors or hospitals or even a nurse in the damned area. He ran to Jaffer who sent a tonga to the other side of town to get one at the earliest. Naseem was saved by the skin of her teeth. This attempted suicide left Shanwaz shaken. Images of Laila came back to him, her lying on a tonga, her body covered in flowers, the hole in the ground into which she disappeared forever. He felt he couldn't relive the tragedy. But he was aware that life had become a burden for his mother. She was born within the walls of the old city, she had grown up there and never left it, and had never known anything but the four streets of Shahi Mohalla. Her world was a miserable shrinking hole where her happiest moments had been when she danced and sang for men in whose eyes she had felt alive, the intoxication of the moment that made her heart beat wildly, those moments of triumph that were hers alone, her feet covered in the bank notes collecting on the floor. What remained of it all? A body that the same men now turned away from. A murdered daughter. A grandchild whose very presence tormented her. Of course, there was also Shanwaz. But Shanwaz was still chasing fantasies of becoming a painter.

A painter? What a strange idea, she thought. Art had replaced religion. What other whim would cross his mind next? Now that he was done with Urdu and English, he had bought himself paints and brushes; he sat up on the roof at sunset and applied himself to sketching the Badshahi. For him, its architectural simplicity was an extraordinary evocation of the presence of the invisible. But it wasn't easy drawing its contours. The most difficult part was really that incredible pink, never ever quite the same, changing with the light, the clouds, the wind. Amused neighbours watched him from their roofs.

'What are you doing Shanwaz?' they cried out, laughing.

Submissive, silent Sana climbed up to the roof terrace with little Aisha in her arms to gawk at her husband dithering before a piece of paper. One day Shanwaz observed her from a distance, sitting on the edge of a seat. He turned away from the Badshahi whose every corner he knew by heart, picked up his pencil and started drawing her. Despite the complexities of the human figure, he was soon caught up in it. Everyday he asked her to sit in the same place without moving until drawing and colours together finally evoked a shadow of something like Sana.

This first portrait of a woman was a revelation. Yes, he was going to paint women. Not just any women, but the dancers of Hira Mandi, their world, their suffering. The world had to know. Society needed to shed its apathy, and to those who didn't even suspect of their existence he needed to show that these women behind Lahore's dilapidated walls deserved respect as much as any others.

The first floor of the house had remained unoccupied since the two aunts had left to be with Allah and his saints. Shanwaz emptied it of the bric-a-brac that had collected there over the years – moth-eaten wall hangings, termite-ridden furniture, all went out the window. Scavenging rag pickers rushed to recover what they could, all that had been chopped, rent, cut up and piled up in big jute bags. Once they had been emptied, the two rooms were thoroughly cleaned, the wooden floors scoured and waxed, and the walls scrubbed and white-washed. The house was coming undone, but Shanwaz hoped to show off this little jewel of Mughal architecture one day. For now, with the little means he had, he was happy just cleaning and refurbishing it to be able to have a place where he could paint, away from the mocking stares of his neighbours.

The news spread through the neighbourhood. Shanwaz, an artist? Most had a good laugh. After all, it was as good as loitering in the streets or getting into drugs like Omar who was now a miserable wreck and could no longer find any muscle on his bones to stick a needle into. Naseem didn't take this sudden passion very seriously. Just another whim that would last a few months before he moved on to something else, she thought. Who in the world would want to see portraits of Hira Mandi's women? He would probably just attract the ire of religious authorities. Islam and figural representation didn't go well together. But Shanwaz showed unbending determination. His personality had changed in the space of a few years. He had undergone a metamorphosis and his dark glare radiated an inner strength. Nothing could stop him. He now knew what his destiny was and he made light of jokes, sarcasm and other threats.

He couldn't yet afford an easel, so he propped his canvas against a chair. He had made it himself with an old bedsheet and four bits of wood. His only expenses were brushes and paints, and they cost him a fortune! But all dreams demanded sacrifices. His first models were the two cousins who still lived there and had moved in with Naseem on the second floor. They didn't take him seriously either. They both sat on chairs and burst into laughter all the time, gesticulating incessantly and jabbering away indefatigably, breaking his concentration. He got angry, but there was no choice, he just had to get used to it.

When the painting was finally done after a few days of clamorous posing, the cousins – who were dying to see the result – came over to take a look at the women daubed onto the canvas. They howled with amazement, then burst out laughing, asking Shanwaz who these hideous creatures were. He stuck to his guns. For him there was an uncanny resemblance. Of course, the lines lacked precision, and the colours were not bright enough, and there was room for improvement, he conceded, but the eyes, yes, the eyes were very real and full of life, the silhouettes reflecting what he saw before him. How dishonest of them, he thought. They refused to recognize themselves for what they were – heavy, pot-bellied, and wilted.

Sana had just given birth to their second daughter, Runi. For Naseem it was a real gift from the gods and she made a beeline for the child. Finally, one that didn't have anything in common with Laila! The poor thing looked like a mistake of nature, having inherited every little aspect of her mother's unpleasant face. Of course Shanwaz was relieved, but having a twin of the one he still had no pleasure in looking at didn't make him any happier. He strove hard to be a husband despite all the difficulties that it represented for him. He had to go far away, farther and farther away, for inspiration, since the images in his mind were now all used up, his memories had faded, and Sana remained as exciting as a dead branch lying by the roadside. One evening when he'd had enough, and was tired with his useless and desperate attempts, he whispered in her ear, 'Do you think you could move a little?'

'Move where? To go where?' She had moaned.

He'd felt at a loss for words, and suddenly very awkward.

'Just move … like a woman …'

She had burst into tears and he was unable to calm her down. Like a miserable, beaten stray dog, that was thrashed; Shanwaz understood that it was hopeless, and he gave up teaching her the most basic bodily gestures, because she only saw shame and ignominy in it, so much so that she decided to no longer go out without the purdah.

He had wanted to be a model husband, but he ended up thinking about the many attractive women around him, ready to be swept up in the throes of passion, and Naseem was the first to encourage him to escape the drudgery of the marital bed. In fact, it did him a world of good. He was more relaxed and he found his inspiration again. At the end of the day, he would receive the models he had undressed the night before, happy to lend their beauty to a man who had made love to them so well.

His paintings sprang to life like arrows coming out of a void and tormented their observers. His phosphorescent-hued colours managed to convey life with all its pain and anguish in one stroke. While his drawing still lacked verve, he put so much of himself in his work that the emotion became increasingly raw to the point that those who once chuckled in front of his paintings, now observed them in silence. They exuded an energy that was not ephemeral or fleeting like a cloud passing through troubled skies. No, this was an insistent energy, injecting its venom into the subconscious until it was almost impossible to get rid of.

Shanwaz was going through an intensely creative period. He painted every evening with the fire of a condemned man, drawing up the vitality of Eastern nights, piling up the canvasses he soon didn't know what to do with.

6

The old city, now symbolized by its two jewels of Mughal architecture – the beautiful ochre-red fort, and the Badshahi – maintained its distance from this world it didn't seem to belong to. It was suffocating behind its enclosure of crumbling stones. Increasingly over-populated, pallid and horridly noisy, it was gasping for air, trying to survive the excesses of its history. And Shanwaz knew nothing of this history. He would have been at a loss to name the monuments and to explain their periods or their styles. There was no city on the subcontinent with as turbulent a past as Lahore. After having seen the reign of Hindu kings, Mughal emperors, Sikh monarchs and British sovereigns, in 1947, at the time of the Partition, she was the capital of a British province, a fortress of the Indian empire and the Paris of the East, a reputation soon lost due to an increasingly conservative Islamic autocracy.

In the midst of their most prestigious Mughal-Victorian style buildings, in the big white library bordering the massive avenue the British called The Mall, a fascinated Shanwaz had thrown himself into reading old books, one of which was the captivating work of a seventeenth century Spanish monk who had passed through this place 'as close as you can get to paradise', describing a 'very clean city, abundantly provided for, but where it was difficult to move around because of the milling crowds, on foot, on camels and on elephants'. Only the elephants had disappeared, thought Shanwaz, replaced in the mid-1960s by the unbearably loud, savage rickshaws that polluted the already suffocating air. The crowds had not changed, a perpetually moving ribbon that nothing could ever stop, not the desperate honking of motorcycles, nor the yells of the tonga-wallahs. But whereas pulsating, tangible and hubbub best described the streets, on the roofs, where the kites took flight during the spring festival, Basant, life went on quietly, a little numbed by the light.

After the muezzin's call under an early morning sun that resembled crumpled tissue paper, when the first tongas were enjoying the emptiness to race down the streets, he had gone to Delhi Gate on foot. From his house a long, narrow street cut across the old city from one end to the other like a knife plunged through a cake full of marshmallows and sugar flowers. Stalls were beginning to open, and poor old people hurriedly took a discrete wash at a public tap. This was the first time in all these years that he had come here, barely a twenty-minute walk away. His readings had led him to discover the existence of a mosque considered to be Pakistan's most beautiful. He didn't dare believe it. For him, the most sumptuous, the most grandiose was the one he had before his eyes all day long, and whose white marble domes sparkled in the full moon. How could the Wazir Khan mosque be as splendid? His insatiable curiosity had led him to go and see for himself this monument built by Wazir Khan, governor of Punjab under Shah Jahan, the Mughal emperor who had left an everlasting mark in history by building the Taj Mahal, the most phenomenal mausoleum in white marble ever constructed for love of a woman. His breath caught before the façade of the Wazir Khan mosque. The blue mosaic designs were so delicate and refined that he was plunged into a state of pure ecstasy. This was the height of perfection in art. How did the human mind even conceive such beauty?

At the entrance, he reflected on the epitaph engraved in stone:

Remove thy heart from the gardens of the world,
and know that this building is the true abode of man.

He took his shoes off to climb the few steps in pink sandstone. In the courtyard, a flight of pigeons drew his gaze to the octagonal minarets covered in fine inlay work in coloured stones. Inside the *mihraab*, the cupolas were like an Eden, decked in the most beautiful flowers ever created. He knelt on the prayer mat and prayed in the priceless intimacy. There was an air of intense plenitude in this holy place. He came out of there at peace with the world.

After being swallowed up by a narrow winding staircase, so dark he couldn't see the streaks of betel that nauseated him, Shanwaz came out and goggled at a city that was even more ochre, more medieval, and whose houses were packed so close together that it was impossible to make out the streets below. The roofs of Lahore were a world suspended between the tumult below and the hope of less foul air above, a place where women abandoned themselves to lust amidst rustling pigeon wings. From this high perch, the Wazir Khan mosque lay below, resplendent like a painting wherein design, proportion and the choice of colours had been mastered to perfection.

Since his fortuitous introduction to art, Shanwaz no longer saw the world with the same eyes. Earlier, things, people, and even life itself were like empty forms. There was nothing he could have slipped into them to lessen his boredom. Now, despite the monotony of the days, there was an intensity in his life. A little music had risen within him, metamorphosed into passion, and once and for all it had pulled him out of the little goldfish bowl he had spent years turning circles in, without any vision of the world other that that deformed by the absence of any perspective. He had become a full-fledged artist without actually becoming a part of the world of art. He had come a long way in a society full of taboos and obscurantism.

After he had read how much attention Fra Sebastian Manrique paid to the splendours of Lahore in the seventeenth century, at a time when the city was bursting with *havelis*, feudal mansions now compressed in urban density, Shanwaz had looked everywhere in the streets for these stately homes, most of which were in a deplorable state, having been abandoned long ago by the Mughal descendants who owned them. One such mansion was the Barood Khana, facing the City Cinema a stone's throw away from Hira Mandi. From the outside you didn't really feel it was there because the walls closely overlapped the constructions around. Only the huge wooden doorway gave any indication of the ancient and refined architecture that lay behind.

An old lady lived there, surrounded by a few faithful servants. She was the widow of a famous poet, and had refused to leave the family haveli even when the rest of the family had left the increasingly seedy neighbourhood to build a villa with all modern conveniences in the new city. She never went out of the haveli. Her only regular visitor to this part of the city was her young, twenty-something grandson, Asif Sahudiqi. He did not care much for the new house his parents had built, with its too-white walls, its garish luxury and western style, and its aseptic ambiance resembling a hospital. Shahi Mohalla was his childhood. He liked its people, its smells, this way of living without social boundaries, each participating in and sharing in the neighbourly life. Shahi Mohalla was a big community, a large family whose charm lay in its strong ancestral traditions.

Shanwaz only knew him by reputation, the two had never met. Since he had left for the other side of the walls, Asif had cut himself off from the daily life of the old city. He was a student at university and came visiting his grandmother only over the weekends when he slept in a room on the last floor of the haveli, lulled by the sounds of the muezzin, and leaned out over the inner garden when the sun came up, where white doves drank water in the marble fountains peacefully.

There was something calming and timeless about the life within the walls of the house. He spent hours smoking pot and listening to music, then ate with the old lady in the afternoons, and left like he had come, without the least worry about life in the increasingly noisy and grimy alleys. He was therefore unaware that a stone's throw from there, an artist was struggling to try and evolve a different vision of society.

Shanwaz, the insatiable explorer who was still working at the cloth factory and picked up his brushes as soon as he got home –, occupied his rare moments of freedom increasing his knowledge. He wondered about the painters in his country. Since the Partition, artists had found it difficult to find their place in an unstable country. Like everything else, art too was stagnating.

One day, seated in the back of a backfiring, belching rickshaw, he set out for Lahore's National Museum, an imposing structure in dull red, built by the English in a bastard style that borrowed from Gothic and Mughal architecture. Its first curator was John Lockwood Kipling, father of the famous Rudyard whose books were still sold in all the book stores. At first Shanwaz was captivated by the Indian miniatures – two entire rows of small paintings of such poetry and refinement that he could not get enough of them. The one showing the sultan Baz Bahadur carrying away the beautiful Roopmati on his white horse, in particular, left him dreamy-eyed for a long time. When he finally reached the big room of Pakistani contemporary art, he stopped in amazement. From the picture rails hung the worst and the best. To him, the worst were the bizarre, abstract signs on gaudy backdrops without harmony or meaning, like unsightly childish doodling which he really couldn't make anything of. But mercifully, right next to the oddities, there bloomed magnificent landscapes in warm colours and soft expressive light and nuanced tones.

He lingered in front of these canvasses that transported him to a world he had been deprived of since his childhood – endless open green spaces stretching into a horizon where one could walk without coming across house, or human: a magical silent, dustless world, the likes of which he had never seen before. The painter's name was Khalid Iqbal.

Shanwaz spent time before each painting, irrespective of whether he liked it or not, to absorb what each painter had wanted to express. There were few human figures, apart from a few portraits without much emotional appeal. Barring a few exceptions, Pakistani painting appeared so limited that he became aware of the originality of his own work within his country's art scene, and felt like he had an open field in front of him. He had his place in this universe.

Shanwaz knew how to read and write, to speak English, he had a respectable job and a growing family – he now had a third daughter, Rami – and was piling up paintings month after month and no longer knew where to stock them. But nothing was moving. The world was still closed to him, and as hostile. Who in the city would finally take an interest in his work? Despite the impatience that sometimes made him rage inwardly, he was certain that time was on his side. Was he not getting better? He was establishing his own style. And now the dancers were all behind him, they were his fan club. After having rejected him for long, they now dreamed of seeing themselves on the fabric framed in wood, flattered at being the seductive artist's muse.

At over thirty, Shanwaz was finally beginning to find his place in Shahi Mohalla. The dancers had found an unusual confidante in him. He listened to them with the tips of his paintbrush. In the beginning, their chatter had alarmed him. They disturbed his work. He lost his much-needed concentration in choosing the right colours, placing the shadows in the right places and finding the right perspective. But slowly he grew accustomed to what he had first seen as prattling women, prone to talking about anything and everything. With time he understood how much better he understood his surroundings through their stories, the laws that governed it, the secular rules that were impossible to transgress, the different castes within what had always appeared to be one big family.

He had been lucky enough to be spared many horrors, because Naseem was from the superior Kanjar caste, amongst the first to have made prostitution a family tradition – in some ways, the nobility of the profession with a genealogy that could be traced to the time of Mughal emperors. In that era, civilization had attained a higher level of refinement. Art in every field demonstrated such a degree of perfection that singers and dancers had uplifted prostitution to the highest level of grace and distinction. In this blessed period, Shahi Mohalla's salons flourished in luxury and elegance, like little palaces opening into the streets. But the arrival of the English was almost fatal for the royal bazaar. With their self-righteous narrow-mindedness, they made prostitution a monster of perversity and never tried to understand Shahi Mohalla beyond their own limited perception of morality. The social hierarchy within the neighbourhood started breaking down. Despite their hypocritical taboos, the English weren't the least numerous or the least ardent clients, but they were the most contemptuous of the dancers, and often mistreated them. The great courtesans slowly disappeared and made way for lower-caste prostitutes. Islam and its mullahs tightened the noose to near-suffocation but they were unsuccessful in eradicating traditions that were so anchored in the city's roots that they could resist for a little more time.

Shanwaz took an avid interest in his models' stories. He was the first to revive the conversation when an oppressive silence settled between them. One day, a dancer with a delicate face and slanted Asian eyes sat before him silently. She had been sent by another of his models. Pretty wisp of a woman, thought Shanwaz, but such sadness in her eyes. She talked only after several sittings.

'It's difficult for me to talk about sorrows and things I have buried so deep inside me that I sometimes forget them,' she said, on the verge of tears.

Gently, slowly, Shanwaz got Chanda to reveal the secrets that made her suffer so. Her mother, Jamila, was not from Shahi Mohalla, but from a poor village a few kilometres from Lahore. When her husband died, Jamila's mother was left alone with nothing but her little daughter, the only thing she could bank on to get them out of their misery. In Pakistan, a young girl could be sold; so she took Jamila to Lahore, and was ignorant enough of the ways of the world to be delighted to find an old lady called Khanum in the old city who accepted the young girl as a bride for her son although she was without a dowry and resources. The mother left, thanking Allah for having placed such a generous woman in her path willing to take in a young girl of fifteen into her house.

Jamila was quick to understand what kind of world she had been abandoned in. Months went by. She was not allowed to see her mother again. The poor worried woman came back to Lahore only to realize in despair that she had settled her daughter into a family of prostitutes. She went away and died of shame. Alone and devastated, Jamila became the prisoner of a clan that used her to make children. Khanum didn't have any daughters, only a son who was given the job of making her pregnant. He gave her one child every year – six daughters and two sons. Chanda was the first, and swiftly removed from her mother, who became the family servant. Chanda's birth was celebrated with great pomp, oil lamps burned everywhere, sweetmeats were distributed to close relatives, and musicians and dancers put up a show that lasted until dawn. Jamila spent her day locked in the kitchen preparing food for the guests. Khanum appropriated Chanda and brought her up as her own child, prohibiting the 'golden egg-laying hen' Jamila from telling the children that she was their mother. Khanum's future was now secure. A prostitute without an heir exposed herself to the worst future. With six girls in hand, she rejoiced and thanked God for having sent her this country girl. She sent Chanda to school and then to high school for two years. The world was changing and clients were becoming more and more demanding. They wanted educated dancers who spoke English, the one condition they had to fulfil to survive in this increasingly tough and fiercely competitive market. But too much education held the risk of their becoming aware of their condition and refusing to come back. Which was what happened with Chanda. After this exposure to the outside world, she understood what the future held for her if she returned to Shahi Mohalla. She rebelled and the crisis reached such proportions that one day Khanum dragged Jamila out of the house and ordered her to scram with her eight children. This was how Chanda learned who her real mother was. It was a rude shock. She had always treated her like a slave. Cornered like that, Chanda had given in to the blackmail and entered the world of prostitution.

Every story added to the misery and the revolt, and made Shanwaz all the more resolute that none of his girls would enter the 'business', as it was now called. Aisha was growing up and would soon be of age for the ring-opening ceremony. Naseem, who had finally overcome the torment that she felt on gazing upon this other Laila who resembled her dead daughter in every respect, had taken the little one under her wing to perfect her education. Aisha went to school and then, like Chanda, spent two years in high school learning English. As soon as she got back home, Naseem called in their neighbour Mustafa to train her in singing and dancing. Aisha had all the trappings of a good courtesan – she was slim and delicate, doll-faced, with intelligent sparkling eyes, and most importantly, blessed with very fair skin, a sign of distinction and refinement that rich clients were keen on. Under her grandmother's guidance, Aisha showed no resistance; the profession did not displease her, she liked dancing and greatly enjoyed singing. Her slightly husky voice filled the air with a soft sensuality.

Naseem was ready to do anything to make Aisha one of Hira Mandi's famous, wealthy and adored dancers. It was a question of survival. Naseem had been forced to cut down her rates to increase her client list which her age had drastically reduced, and this was reflected in the social status of those who climbed her stairs. She was loath to be professional, faced with dirty, frustrated individuals stinking of sweat. She was tired, and more worn out, more fragile with every passing day. And she watched Aisha grow with impatience, sometimes bordering on hysteria.

Aisha was a shy, gentle child, terrified of her father. He was cold and distant with her. The older she grew, the more he could see his darling sister in her. She would soon be as old as Laila was when he had gone into her room for the first time to possess her. He became so uneasy at the idea that he avoided even looking at his daughter. Aisha's pain was as great as her incomprehension. No one had ever spoken to her about Laila. Why dig up old wounds when life was already so difficult? She was particularly hurt when she saw her father's tenderness for her little sisters. But behind this indifference which in fact masked his own pain, Shanwaz refused to imagine Aisha on the Hira Mandi stage. The very thought that what happened to Laila could happen to her drove him mad with anxiety. But what could he do to stop Naseem? In the Kanjar caste ruled by unrelenting matriarchy, she had all the power in the family, and men were but second-class citizens whose opinion was never asked for.

Life in Shahi Mohalla drew its strength from tradition. Nobody dared break away from the basic neighbourhood rules. And although he was an educated, independent man, Shanwaz could protest but not oppose. He did not yet have the means to take care of his mother. He was barely earning enough for his own family and for his paints. The house was ready to crumble and fall, and Sana was expecting their fourth child.

7

The suffocating humidity of the August monsoon made even the slightest chore unbearable. Even when it wasn't raining, the air was so full of moisture that it felt like being in a steam bath. These horrid summers were dreaded by everyone in the old city where few had the means to have fans installed. The walls of the house seeped in moisture and smelt of rot, and pestilential odours rose from the gutters where men crouched for their daily needs. The street resembled a court of miracles – handicapped beggars, cripples rolling in a ball on the ground, tramps in the last shreds of a shalwar kameez, and emaciated drug addicts with transparent skin who had nowhere to shield themselves from the oppressive heat that hung on long after the sun had set. This grovelling misery, multiplying like unhealthy vermin that no one did anything to check, disturbed Shanwaz. From the outside the old city within its misshapen walls looked like a junkyard for all of society's most depraved – dealers, prostitutes, pimps and of course, Shi'as, as rejected as the Christians. The only ones who dared enter here were the bourgeois in need of excitement, ready to mix with the riff-raff at the cost of their virtue, politicians who by day proudly brandished the Quran, and by night the bank notes that they showered on the dancers.

In the name of Islam, in other words, before elections or on the eve of Ramadan, the government came to peek at the lewd morals of the old city and its charms, and Shahi Mohalla in particular. Power, whether in the hands of the army or in a civilian government, wasn't very different in its treatment of Shahi Mohalla – violence and blind repression condemned its inmates to adversity. Until the day winds of revolt gushed through the dark alleys.

Some neighbourhood personalities met in a dark square one evening to discuss how to impose their right to live like any other citizen of the country. Amongst them was a notorious gangster, a certain Mahmud Sahib, a tall, good-looking man with a disturbing presence. Shanwaz also attended this meeting. His reputation as the destroyer of an alienating political regime was well-established. At thirty-three, he had had time to mould his political consciousness. After twenty three years of existence, his country was a nation without a state, whereas India had become a parliamentary democracy in the same time. How had they ever believed that Pakistan, confined within artificial boundaries, could magically engender a regulated, civic state? In fact nobody had ever thought about how the country should be governed. The triumph of faith had brought success. But not a single government after Jinnah's death had managed to establish a viable system to make the original dream a reality – that of a real country for the sub-continent's Muslims. The army could not offer much more than martial law and emergency regimes

– democracy was equally unattainable for them and they stumbled like their predecessors in trying to create a real state. Caught in the stranglehold of harsh reality, and subjugated by despotic dictatorships, Pakistanis struggled and survived as they could.

In the old city, Mahmud Sahib had decided to act. He proposed the creation of an Association of Artists of Shahi Mohalla to fight the oppression; then he declared himself president and nominated Shanwaz as secretary. The aim of the association was to protect and defend the neighbourhood.

'Whether it's the society outside or the police inside these walls, we are outcasts for them all,' he proclaimed in his stentorious voice to the crowd gathered at his feet. 'We must fight to stop this contempt that makes our children so ashamed.'

Shanwaz agreed. Some days before Ramadan, he entered the High Court of Lahore to meet a lawyer whom Jaffer had introduced to him. He wanted to have dancers and musicians recognized as workers so they could enjoy the same rights as any other business-person in the country, and to have the ban on their activities during the fasting month lifted. The case was examined by a court of law which recognized that there was no legal text preventing the artists from doing what they did during Ramadan. Shanwaz had the text printed and a thousand photocopies made and pasted all over Shahi Mohalla.

On the eve of the month of Ramadan, dozens of police vehicles encircled the old city to prevent anyone from entering. Armed men entered Shahi Mohalla to stop the salons from opening. But they weren't prepared for the thousands of people who poured into the streets, shouting and chanting, determined to stand up to them. The protesters sat down in the middle of the streets and on the pavements. Musicians began to play and dancers began to dance, brandishing the text under the noses of the policemen, most of whom were illiterate. But there was nothing doing. The orders had come from above, much above the law.

And the scenario repeated itself during the thirty fasting days. Sometimes the stand-off between the police and protesters degenerated and those demanding their rights, text in hand, ended up being beaten.

Shanwaz had to go into hiding during this time. The police, at first taken by surprise by the revolt, had not taken long in starting their search for the individuals responsible for the chaos. They had used all means of coercion on those they suspected of knowing who the guilty parties were, and had recovered some names in the end. But how were they to get their hands on a fugitive in the labyrinth of these alleys?

On *Eid*, the religious ceremony that marked the end of Ramadan, Shanwaz came back to his rooftop terrace, and was spellbound as he contemplated the thousands of pilgrims on the burning tiles of the Badshahi, that pink and white highlight of Mughal art, built around a hair from Prophet Muhammad's beard. When the muezzin launched into prayer from the top of the minarets, his voice was quickly drowned by the sound of sixty thousand pairs of knees meeting the floor, then sixty thousand chests murmuring Allah's name. After around twenty minutes, Islam's most solemn ceremony ended in a few canon shots while the pilgrims hugged each other, wishing the best to all in the year to come, because the situation in East Pakistan was deteriorating.

East Bengal was violently demanding its independence. The new preoccupations of the authorities ended the manhunt. Shanwaz could finally resurface.

The loss of East Bengal on 16 December 1971 was a terrible blow to Pakistan, further humiliated by India's backing of the East Bengali people. The country's morale was at an all-time low. Religion, the founding principle of the country, had not succeeded in creating unity, and their very faith in the survival of the country was shaken. Jinnah's dream was disintegrating – a dream that was never realised because sixty million Muslims still lived in India. Pakistanis were angered by the images of the capitulation shown on TV. Hysterical mobs descended into the streets, their self-esteem and pride hurt by scenes of the defeated General Niazi embracing his Indian counterpart, General Aurora. Like his fellow countrymen, Shanwaz couldn't believe his eyes when he saw the traditional exchange of swords with much embracing! He was deeply mortified, even more so because Indian newspapers did not hesitate to qualify Pakistan as a 'fictitious nation which should never have seen the light of day', stoking a hate that always lingered just under the surface.

Zulfikar Ali Bhutto, a pugnacious man with rebellious charisma, took advantage of the breach in the general mayhem and became president of a sick Pakistan, maimed by war and debased by defeat. In the absence of a Constitution, he took oath of office as the first civilian in history to take the reins of an administration under martial law. Winds of hope accompanied his arrival. At thirty, he was already the youngest minister in the country. He became a hero when he came out of the prison he had been thrown into by General Ayub, and crowds jostled to cheer him when he created the famous PPP, the Pakistan People's Party – a lifeline for the poor, the pariahs and the ill-treated. The inhabitants of Lahore's old city were overcome with emotion – it had been so long since they could even dare to hope for any betterment in their lives. Was it possible that this man would understand their problems and let them live in peace? Would the magnetic Bhutto, the unlikely saviour, know how to pull them out of the obscenity of their despair? Would the millstone that hung around their necks since Jinnah's death come off and pave the way to a better future?

Shanwaz feverishly followed the developments within the freshly constituted team. A year later, Bhutto relinquished the presidential chair to become prime minister while preserving all his powers and had a Constitution voted into place that guaranteed an independent judiciary, a structured economy, a parliamentary government, freedom of the press, religious freedom and civil rights for all.

Those years brought respite to Shahi Mohalla. There was less repression, a more relaxed relationship with the authorities, and the dancers were able to take up their profession again. Rich clients who had for long been deterred by the neighbourhood's nefarious ambiance, were seen there again.

Naseem decided it was a favourable period to organize her granddaughter Aisha's ring ceremony. Shanwaz lost all sleep and appetite at the thought. He found no solace in anything. Sana was surprised. She put it down to a father not being able to bear the thought of his daughter growing up. She could never have imagined that behind it all lay memories of Laila whom she remembered only vaguely. They had never been friends – Laila didn't have time for her neighbour's vacuous eyes. Besides, they didn't belong to the same world, and met only rarely because one came alive at night while the other slept. Sana, whose naivete protected her from taboos, was serenely waiting for her daughter's entry into the world of dancers. In fact she was even quite proud of it. She looked at her with curiosity but never really thought about it. Sometimes one wondered if she even understood what it meant to 'enter the business'. Naseem had taken her daughter and appropriated her. Aisha lived with her grandmother and so escaped her little sisters, and their cries – the latest so far, Naika, was only a few months old – and the pathetic mess that reigned in the puny rooms of the last floor. Sana did not overly preoccupy herself with order and cleanliness, preferring to rely on an old servant to whom everybody gave chores, not realizing that the old woman had lost her marbles and didn't clean much anymore.

For the third time in her life, Naseem had the red and gold shamiana erected in the square behind the house. It was decorated on the inside with thousands of tiny mirrors whose magical reflections danced all around the tent. She invited dancers and transvestites, all dressed like multicoloured butterflies, and let it be known through word of mouth, which worked so well in Shahi Mohalla, to attract Lahore's richest and most depraved men. The ceremony took place late at night. It started to rain, long glassy needles that broke on the roof and transformed every house into a ghost ship buffeted by angry transparent waves. The madly beating rain did not disturb the ceremony under the shamiana. The impatience of the gathering had reached its paroxysm when finally, gliding between the veils protecting her, Aisha made an unforgettable appearance. The murmur of deja-vu went through the crowd. For those who still remembered Laila, she was an eerie replica of a distant past. A wave of unease rippled through them like a shiver through damp air.

Shanwaz did not want to be there for a repetition of the tragedy. But Naseem always had the last word. Standing in a corner of the shamiana, he began to tremble when two black eyes enveloped him in darkness. His eyes followed the hands that disappeared into a fugitive and boundless night. His heart reopened like a flower under a hardy sun. His whole body went up in flames and drops of sweat dribbled down inside his clothes, like the long needles of rain living out their absurd lives outside. Aisha's silhouette disappeared behind a mist of pain and Laila appeared in the graceful, swirling dance gestures. When the two images merged, Shanwaz felt his body burn. He stumbled and fled to his room, locked himself in and fell on the bed, his head full of silent wails, the cries absorbed by the emptiness. Sana found him there lying in a semi-coma that she took for deep sleep. He never asked who had broken his daughter's ring. Naseem's satisfied smile the next day spoke volumes of the fortune she had pocketed.

Under the large, dense summer sun, Lahore's pulse suddenly quickened. Zulfikar Ali Bhutto's policies gave so much hope that the walled city's inhabitants became unfailing supporters of the new leader. Mythical words like 'democracy' and 'freedom', that were almost metaphysical concepts for most Pakistanis, filled newspapers. '*Roti, Kapra, Makaan*' – bread, clothes and home – Bhutto repeated, and these simple needs became the war cry of the PPP. The basics that millions of poor didn't have access to. 'Muslims prostrate themselves before Allah, but in Pakistan, the poor prostrate themselves before the rich!' Bhutto would go on. 'Stand up! Don't crawl before others! You are human beings and you have rights!' These exhortations gave a tremendous boost to his popularity. Never since Jinnah had Pakistanis flocked through cities and villages to hail one of their leaders joyously. 'There is no divine law that condemns only us Pakistanis to poverty!' The new messiah went everywhere to deliver his message of justice. There was no more fear and suspicion, and for some time the air was filled with a surreal confidence in the future.

For some weeks, there had been much agitation in Hira Mandi, just in front of City Cinema, and people came to watch out of curiosity. The Barood Khana, the old haveli whose architecture had always fascinated Shanwaz, had just buried its owner, Asif Sahudiqi's grandmother. Asif was then around thirty years old, and he decided to start restoring the inheritance that the old lady had left him with. No other family member wanted the cumbersome construction in the state that it was in. 'Only a mad man would want to settle down amidst the rabble, the dirt and the stench of the Mughal hovels,' is what they thought in Lahore's chic neighbourhoods. Asif thought exactly the opposite.

He was the black sheep in an ultra-conservative family that belonged to the twenty-two clans that had controlled the industries and the banks since the country's creation. They were thus becoming sickeningly rich, and he had just caused a stir by rallying to Bhutto's cause. He set himself up as a defender of social and economic reform, and opened the PPP's first office just in front of the Barood Khana. In no time the building, with a red, green and black flag fluttering above it, was full of those who wanted their party card. Asif would go there every day. His security staff of discreetly armed bodyguards was obliged to contain the excited mob, impatient to know the latest measures the government had taken in its favour.

Asif was not married. He refused the pretty damsels his parents presented to him – alliances made to reinforce the wealth and power of the family. These women were of no interest to him, no more than the money that he already didn't know what to do with. His paternal grandfather had made his fortune in textiles. Asif worked part-time for one of his branches in Lahore, but the world of business disgusted him from the day he became aware of the working conditions of his labourers – their slave-like existence, their slaving children working twelve hours a day for a few rupees which were barely enough to feed them. His idealism of the affluent was scandalized at the disdain with which these people were treated – barefoot and bare-chested, eaten away by gnawing pain and hunger. He himself had always been spared any worries, attending the best schools, having a plethora of servants who prostrated themselves before him and touched his feet before walking backwards out of his presence – a custom inherited from the Mughals.

Asif Sahudiqi had welcomed Bhutto's arrival with great relief. Under his leadership, Pakistan would finally enter the ranks of civilized nations, respecting the rights of all and perhaps taking care of its cultural heritage which had so far been scorned by governments that refused to accept the existence of other civilizations before Islam. Asif knew that Jinnah's religious state, still half-plunged in serfdom and profoundly uneducated, mutilating history in school textbooks and constantly undoing the political entity it was supposed to serve, had not stopped transforming the country into a cultural void. Educated in the bosom of maternal grandparents open to art and poetry, he was an aesthete with a predetermined destiny – to carry the flame of the past like the symbol of a growing, civilized nation. Beauty fascinated him in all its forms. His restoration of the haveli was the first step in affirming his ideas, an example that would awaken other vocations, he hoped. But he was confronted with a tremendous obstacle – no artisan in Pakistan was capable of making replicas of the antique work.

In the past twenty-five years, nobody had cared for ancient architecture, and it had been destroyed shamelessly, with bricks and cement slapped in where needed. Those who could imitate the ancient artwork were either dead or had left for India. Asif understood the danger faced not just by the magnificent monuments of Lahore, but by all of Pakistan's heritage, from the forts of Sindh to the Bhawalpur palace. How ironic for a country that proclaimed its Islamic identity out loud and declared itself the inheritor of Mughal power! It was these very Mughal monuments, the fort, the Badshahi, the Shalimar gardens, and Jahangir's tomb that were being left to fall into disrepair for lack of education. They were seen as being of no use. So who would demand their upkeep? He protested against this very Islamic attitude where nothing was of interest or made any sense apart from the sacred sands of Arabia.

To lend more weight to his struggle, Asif joined the Punjab Provincial Assembly without any illusions about the highly limited role that he would get to play. In a country where everything had to be built from scratch, heritage conservation was hardly a priority. In fact, even Bhutto had not thought it necessary to create a ministry for cultural affairs. But Asif wasn't giving up. If the way had to be shown, he would start with his own house.

He supervised the work for months, chose the labourers himself after testing their skills, taking the time to explain to them what he wanted and how. While waiting for the ground floor rooms to be done up, he took up quarters on the last floor of the haveli, in the room his grandmother had occupied while she was alive. For months, he spent his days between the PPP offices and the work in the house which progressed at a characteristically slow but healthy Pakistani pace. He lived a radically different life from the worldly existence he had known until then in his parents' house. He was alone now. None of his friends ventured into the Mughal city. Most couldn't understand his desire to return to what they saw as a finished past. Why spend so much money to restore dilapidated walls when he had the means to have a villa in the middle of a big garden that would do justice to his money? But Asif did not justify himself. It was too early. These feudal families who were so scared of Bhutto and his politics, would for long prevent the development of a humane and humanist society.

8

Seated in his workshop, his head buried in his hands, Shanwaz reflected on the misery of reality. He had touched the bottom of the abyss. Mr Bhutto's fine, noble principles would for long remain ineffectual in the medieval world of the old city. He had come face to face with the horror of hate brought on by the vilest of ill deeds. The evening before, just before night fell, a delirious adolescent had knocked on his door, asking him to come quickly.

'An accident, an accident,' he kept repeating in shock, unable to say more.

Two streets from there, Shanwaz followed him up the stairs of a house he knew well. One of his four cousins lived there. Her stormy life had taken its toll on her like a beast of burden under the repeated blows of her troubled destiny. At the door, he heard cries like women whose throats were being slit open.

His heart stopped. The boy, still delirious, was now terrified as he opened the door. Shanwaz went towards the room the screams were coming from. Many women were gesticulating crazily, weeping and moaning over a body laid out on the bed. Shanwaz saw his cousin amongst them. When she moved to let him pass, what he saw was so unbearable that he had to close his eyes for a moment and was afraid to open them. He broke into a cold sweat that froze his spine.

'Help us! Please, help us!' his hysterical cousin cried out.

Her daughter, Shurma, lay on the bed, a sixteen-year-old beauty of whom Shanwaz had made many portraits. He took infinite pleasure in painting her, her skin was so fine and delicately gilded and her grey-blue eyes gave an exquisite luminosity to her face, so rare even in the most beautiful women.

But now her face on the white pillow had melted away. All that remained was a hideous, monstrous red mask. Her right eyelid was a mass of flesh stuck to her eyeball. The purulent left one hung over a blind eye. The nose had been gnawed to the bone. Tears flowed from the dead eyes as Shurma sobbed in silence.

Finally, getting a hold on himself, Shanwaz took things into hand.

'Get a tonga,' he ordered the women. 'We have to get her to a hospital.'

The cousin hid Shurma's face under a light veil while Shanwaz helped the women carry her to the tonga. The journey to the hospital was an ordeal for the half-conscious young girl, and her scorched throat made hoarse sounds like an old woman in pain. The nurses put her on a stretcher, took her into an immense room and left her on a bed amidst fifty other people under the pallid light. A large, sprightly woman came over, her bulky person wrapped in a white coat. It was the surgeon.

'Acid, wasn't it?' she asked, already certain. She looked at the face with profound revulsion.

'Do you know who it was?' she asked, turning towards the cousin.

'No! She doesn't want to say.'

But Shanwaz knew. No doubt a jealous or rejected lover settling scores. Acid attacks were a recent development that were becoming frequent. It was the revenge of the cowardly, of savages, base men who gave vent to their animal instincts, knowing their actions would go unpunished. Pakistani law was deplorably discriminatory towards women. Even after lodging a complaint, they had no chance of being heard. In fact, they never complained for fear of reprisals. Shanwaz watched the woman in the white blouse, defeated.

'We doctors have the right to take testimonies of our patients but most men don't want to get involved. As for policemen, it's just another opportunity to pocket bribes and put the matter under wraps. The women in this country are objects, things, and what happens to them is unimportant,' she said, outraged, helplessly stroking the burnt girl's hair.

'Doctor, what can you do?' asked the cousin, tears streaking her face, her cheeks dark with the kohl running from her eyes.

'Treat her to prevent infections, but for the rest, unfortunately, nothing can be done. Her face has been destroyed. Even plastic surgery would not help much. A little perhaps to soften the horror in the eyes of others. And that's a lot already.'

Shanwaz listened, appalled at the ineffectiveness of medicine and the futility of laws. For Shurma, this was worse than death. A long moan rang out from deep within her. She too had heard. Her desire to die must be so great right now, thought Shanwaz.

'How did this happen?' he asked her in a murmur choked with emotion.

He closed his eyes, unable to look at the frightening face. Shurma had trouble breathing. The air that passed through her lungs made her suffer, and she couldn't find the right words.

'In the street,' the cousin answered. 'We found her unconscious in the street. People said that a man came up to her with a glass in his hand and threw the contents on her before running away. But nobody will give his name. Not even Shurma.'

Distressed by the tragedy, Shanwaz returned home where his entire family was waiting for him apprehensively. The news had spread through the neighbourhood. It wasn't the first time such an attack had taken place. The slightest protest from a woman was seen as a rebellion that deserved to be punished. Naseem had always feared men's resentment, knowing well that they didn't beat about the bush when their pride was wounded. All the more because acid was the easiest and the cheapest arm to procure. All sorts of little shops used it. A tall glass of the infernal liquid sold over the counter for just a few rupees. Now Naseem was scared for her pretty and desirable Aisha, whom men fought over. Diplomacy would have to be employed so as not to upset anyone. In the salon she had reopened for her granddaughter, she instructed the musicians to be watchful and ready to throw any client out if he showed himself to be impatient or aggressive.

Shanwaz locked himself up in his workshop on the first floor of the house. The room had become cramped from the number of canvasses that filled it, all facing the walls, piled one over the other. He didn't know what to do with them and he was losing hope of seeing them anywhere else other than in this cheerless place. He looked for one of Shurma's portraits. Her burnt face had so traumatized him that all memory of her face had vanished. He found it at last. The large light eyes set in such splendour … how could all of it disappear forever in one short instant? He sat and stared at the painting for long, moved as though he were in mourning a loved one. Now Shurma's life would be hell. No longer of any use to her mother who was crying more over her own bad luck, she would end up being rejected by all with nowhere to go. What could he do to help her? Shanwaz had no answer. Could he sell her painting for a lot of money and give her the financial aid she needed? But who would want the painting? Who would want all these paintings being devoured by humidity, chewed upon by mice, and whose bad quality paint was already beginning to chip? The years were going by. The desolate thought made his stomach knot. His life was sinking into monotonous platitudes. A long, bleak progression from the moment he stepped out of bed in the morning to start yet another cheerless day, harrowing work, a melancholic evening, crossing the same streets that stank more with every passing day, the terrible stench of rot that enveloped everything: the houses, the people. He was filled with relentless despair. He couldn't live like this any more, surrounded by a family devoid of love. Sana was obsessed with her children, and Naseem only thought of how to make the most of Aisha. As soon as he saw the day break, he got up and crept out of the house like a thief. When he got back in the evening, he would shut himself up in his workshop, even if he couldn't find the will to paint, and went up to his place only once everyone had gone to sleep. This cruel lack of love compounded the giddy emptiness of the days. He was no longer interested in sleeping with the dancers. Of course, he did need the physical exertion without which he would have exploded in anger. But now the blood beating in his veins made empty echoes, a vulgar pleasure, a butcher's rapture.

When he took the time to explore Lahore, Shanwaz pondered why Islamic architecture of the Great Mughals hadn't survived their demise. Pakistan had fallen to the lowest degree of cultural destitution. Everything was deteriorating tragically. The barely ready Grand Trunk Road below Shalimar Gardens was already spewing pollution onto the now colourless flowerbeds. The hundred-year old trees were dead, the canals dry, the four hundred water fountains were hushed and the white marble cascades had dried out.

Shanwaz watched bitterly as the dirt of the world desecrated Emperor Shah Jahan's work. Since the Partition, art had disappeared from the life of the country, as artists had fled the oppression of a religion that had turned hostile to them. Over twenty-five years had gone by, and the timorous creators were expressing themselves with restraint. Painters had lost the spirit of their Mughal ancestors and refused to copy the West. Every time he visited the museum, Shanwaz was convinced that his paintings could fill the empty rails. Lahore, a world apart due to its prodigious past, had established itself as Pakistan's cultural capital and Bhutto's more liberal policies had encouraged a number of artists. Lahore experienced a restorative awakening, a jolt, enthusiasm. Dancers, musicians, and actors flocked to the only place where their work found resonance. As a symbol of this effervescence, the Alhamra Art Centre for contemporary art was constructed on the Mall in red brick, reminiscent of Mughal architecture. One day, as he passed by, Shanwaz saw an immense poster on the façade announcing the exhibition of the painter, Khalid Iqbal. The name was etched in his memory. The artist's work was a universe of infinite green areas stretching into a horizon without houses or humans, an extraordinary world without noise and dust, such as he would never have the opportunity to see.

He went in. In all his life he had never seen a room of such imposing bareness. Just a few dozen paintings on snow white walls bathed in a light that seemed to come from nowhere, giving the room a magical, surreal air. Shanwaz walked in, intimidated by the solemnity of the place where all one could do was admire the paintings of an artist of incomparable talent. With immense pleasure, he walked slowly from painting to painting, taking his time to study each of them. He was alone in a silence conducive to meditation, and so lost he was in the colours that he didn't hear a man walk up to him. When he did notice him, it gave him a start. The man greeted him.

'You seem interested.'

Without hesitation, Shanwaz expressed his admiration for the paintings, 'It's stupendous work! An extraordinary journey through a world I have never seen.'

'I am glad you like my work.'

Shanwaz was confused for an instant, not having recognized the artist, then he took his hand and shook it warmly. He looked at this small man with thinning grey hair, and eyes that shone with such intelligence and kindness, and he was so overwhelmed that he lost his voice. Khalid Iqbal asked him questions. Intimidated, Shanwaz didn't dare admit to being a painter. Then, suddenly aware that this was perhaps a once-in-a-lifetime opportunity, he made a very awkward attempt at doing so. It was the first time he was talking about his painting to someone outside his entourage. He knew the taboos that came with mentioning Shahi Mohalla, and didn't know how to start. But Khalid Iqbal's benevolent gaze helped him begin to recount his life. Droplets of sweat slithered off his forehead. He felt the shame of being seen as a prostitute's son well up deep within him. The shame that had never left him since the day he had tried to find a job outside the walls of the enclosure that he was not expected to leave.

'Come, let's sit,' said Khalid Iqbal, taking him by the arm.

They took a seat on a bench in the garden inside. Now filled with confidence, Shanwaz spoke for long. When he had finished, Khalid Iqbal looked at him with great interest.

'I would like to see your paintings. When can I come to visit?'

Shanwaz, exhausted by the effort, couldn't believe his ears.

'When? But whenever you like, of course!'

9

When he arrived at the exhibition hall, Shanwaz noticed that nine of the thirty-four canvasses had been taken down and placed on the floor, facing the wall. He turned towards one of the guards.

'It's the Alhamra managers. They came last evening,' explained the man. 'Some were angry. They asked me to take down the indecent paintings.'

Shanwaz kept his cool, but inside he was boiling with rage. While he was expecting heated reaction to his first exhibition, he hadn't thought the organizers themselves would become judgemental. The preview was in less than two hours.

His meeting with Khalid Iqbal six months ago had been like a gust of fresh air in his life. The painter had been true to his word and had come to see his paintings. Shanwaz had sorted through his work and ruthlessly removed what he considered mediocre or unfruitful. Amongst the ones he was most proud of, were several large portraits of Shurma.

Khalid had examined everything without uttering a word. His silence played havoc on Shanwaz's nerves. With the unbearable feeling of being stripped naked, he had waited for the axe to fall. He was sweating profusely and his wet hands were having trouble grabbing the canvasses. When Khalid Iqbal finally opened his mouth, Shanwaz was on the verge of fainting. The artist was impressed by the quality of the work, but most of all, its strength and emotion reflected the talent of a well-established artist.

As president of the Association of Pakistani Painters, Khalid Iqbal suggested his colleagues look at Shanwaz's work. They all concluded enthusiastically that it had to be exhibited. And what better place to introduce a young artist than the Alhamra, an institution that had in just a few years created a niche for itself in the media and amongst the public as avant-garde? His mentor's generosity did not stop here. Khalid Iqbal nominated Shanwaz to suceed him as professor at Lahore's National College of Art. He was getting too old for the job. Shanwaz accepted without any hesitation. His life blossomed overnight. He was finally living a real life. His head spun with a euphoria he had only ever experienced with opium; then anxiety took over a few days before the start of the exhibition. Although he was the painter, Shanwaz was not the only one being thrown into the lion's den of critics. The women of Hira Mandi would also take the dreaded test of being thrown into the spotlight. A terrible responsibility. He had taken care to get permission from each of them to exhibit their portraits. All had accepted, seeing it as an opportunity to escape the old walls and reveal their painful existence to the world. And he had promised to share all profits from the sales with them, if there were any …

Shanwaz couldn't understand what was unacceptable in the censored paintings and was outraged at this inelegant behaviour. And to do this to him on the very evening of the preview without even consulting him! He picked up the paintings in anger and was putting them back on their rails when some members of the association entered. They were shocked at this treatment of an artist's work, and asked to meet an Alhamra official. Playing the role of the civil servant to perfection, the man explained that the censored paintings could be controversial as they were disrespectful to Islamic principles. And, seeing that they had been placed back on the wall, he ordered Shanwaz to remove them. The association members surrounded him. Since when did civil servants meddle in the arts? The man was taken aback and called for the director of the Alhamra. Things got heated up. The director finally gave the reasons for the censorship. To begin with, the paintings represented prostitutes. Moreover, they were not veiled. Finally, one of the women had been recognized by someone at the Alhamra. Appalled by these flimsy excuses, Shanwaz flatly refused to take the nine canvasses down.

'Very well,' replied the director. 'In that case, the exhibition is cancelled!'

It was almost time for the preview to begin. Outside, the first visitors had already arrived. An official went out and announced that there would be no exhibition, without explaining why. The public was surprised and bewildered. One of the members of the Association of Painters took the stage to denounce the improper role of those who, despite being mere gallery managers, pretended to have authority over an artist's work. The word censorship caused a great deal of agitation in the ever-increasing numbers in the public, as well as amongst the numerous media persons who had come for the event. The snap judgement had hit Shanwaz hard. The criticism had hit him where it hurt most, the shame that ceaselessly surged from the depths of his soul. But he was soon pulled out of his thoughts by the cries and demonstrations of the thickening crowds at the doors. Outraged that they could not access the exhibition, the people demanded that the work be exhibited outside the gallery.

Shanwaz and his colleagues immediately took down the paintings, brought them out and placed them against the outer walls. Everybody applauded Shanwaz for his talent and courage. The public milled about for an hour to admire these women that no artist had ever dared paint. Journalists fell over each other to interview him. There was such a hubbub in front of the Alhamra that the police arrived, and immediately gave the order to wrap up the canvasses and pushed the crowd back, forcing it to disperse quite quickly. Nobody protested.

But the press had a field day the next day. The Alhamra officials were not spared on any account. Not for their intolerance, or their ignorance, or their stupidity. Entire pages were covered with the censored paintings and the face of the painter who had been insulted, for all Pakistan to see. This was a windfall for intellectuals who could finally launch the debate on art in an Islamic country. Some journalists had been outraged by the reasons given by the officials, as uncultured as they were narrow-minded. One of the paintings, a landscape, had been censored on the excuse that the Badshahi could be seen through the windows, in the background. The mosque was empty, as were the apartments, but as one of the censors retorted, everybody knew that prostitutes lived in these apartments. Therein Islam was insulted. An art critic went even farther. He spoke of the Italian Renaissance painter, Raphael, who used his mistresses as models to represent the Virgin Mary. 'His Madonnas are splendid, and full of religious devotion. It would be totally absurd for someone to attack Raphael for having openly cheated on his wife. The censored paintings do not represent the women of Hira Mandi as objects of desire, but as human beings who are aware of their status. There is not an iota of eroticism in these paintings, not a hint of sexual provocation. These portraits express feelings of profound sadness, of disillusionment, and of tragedy.'

Thirty-seven years of darkness wiped out in less than twenty-four hours. Thrust under the limelight with such haste, Shanwaz had still not fully come to terms with the spectacular spot of luck that had pushed his life into the front pages of newspapers. All of Lahore was talking about him. His story coloured the pages of big Pakistani dailies. 'Death of an exhibition', 'Polemic surrounding a star-crossed painter', 'Oppressive bureaucracy', 'Rejected reality', editorials screamed.

Shanwaz was happy to have stirred the hornet's nest. From that day on he didn't have a day's rest. For weeks, journalists and buyers hurried to his workshop, much to the amazement of his family and the entire neighbourhood who had always taken him for a simpleton, a capricious dreamer, a well-meaning utopian. The neighbours observed the strangers with suspicious curiosity. To the guests who asked him how he chose his subjects, he responded that he simply painted the life around him. He saw himself as an artist with a mission who could not ignore the social situation in Pakistan with its various forms of exploitation.

'The existence of these prostitutes is as much a part of reality as that of the poor, the sick, the un-loved,' he rapped out.

The more subtle minds started a real discussion on a society that drove its women to prostitution instead of protecting them. Shanwaz had opened a breach and had never imagined that so many people in a single, sudden surge would rush in to fill it. With fame came money. Between the sale of his paintings and his job as professor, Shanwaz couldn't believe his eyes when he counted the wads of money that he hid under a plank of his workshop floor. He was true to his word, sharing the profits from the sales of the paintings with his models. This made them flock to him like flies. He didn't know how to get rid of them. They were all ready to pose for him in exchange for unforgettable nights of pleasure. He was flattered, but refused.

In the flow of emotions that had submerged him in the days gone by, the greatest joy was that of having sold Shurma's portraits to a rich businessman. It was an excuse to visit the young girl he hadn't seen since she had left the hospital. He found her alone, burrowed into the floor in the darkest room in the apartment. Her head, posed on a beautiful body that disappeared into the shreds of a *shalwar kameez*, was invisible, hidden under a fine black veil. Her mother had put her in here, like a bag of rubbish to be thrown out. Shanwaz went up to her and spoke to her in a low voice to avoid alarming her. She started, then cowered low. Her dead eyes behind the veil had imprisoned her in a night without end. When she understood who had come into the room, she sighed hoarsely. In a hollow, barely audible groan she confided that her mother would come when the clients were about to arrive. She would drag her daughter to the bedroom, take off her clothes, spray her with cheap perfume, and then cover her face with a thick cloth which she attached firmly. So when the men saw her sumptuous, young, attractive body, they ardently fell upon her, indifferent to the monster hidden under the fabric. Business was booming, so the mother had left to live elsewhere with a man she had attracted with her earnings. A neighbour had been paid to bring her one meagre meal a day. Not wanting to twist the knife in her indelible wounds, Shanwaz didn't mention the sales of the paintings. He couldn't tell her that her once beautiful face had earned a lot of money and that it was for her. How would she have kept it or even benefited from it, anyway? Her mother would have pocketed it soon enough. Shanwaz remembered what the doctor had said about plastic surgery. Maybe with this money, he could have her operated on to give her a less wretched face in the eyes of others.

While Shanwaz experienced the metamorphosis of a life outside the old walls, Mahmud Sahib had ordered his men to find the aggressor of Shurma. Although a goon and a pimp, he did live by some principles. If a man wanted to settle scores with a bitch, let him do it in the open and not flee like a coward once the dastardly act had been committed. Besides, protecting the neighbourhood women was a large chunk of his bread and butter. If he did not intervene when they needed it, they wouldn't trust him any more and would refuse to pay the tax he levied on them. With the attack on Shurma, Shahi Mohalla had lost one of its most beautiful women. It meant less money earned for all, and him in particular. Women like her perpetuated the traditions of Hira Mandi, attracting clients from Dubai, the Emirates, and Saudi Arabia. The ultra-rich petrol princes came to Lahore, enthused by tales of their beauty and their savoir-faire. New salons spawned under Bhutto's more liberal regime. Hira Mandi was bubbling with an effervescence it had not known in many years. Shanwaz's fame had played its part in it of course. The press had contributed to the renown of the dancers by putting their pictures on their front pages.

Mahmud Sahib lived in a minuscule house at the end of an alley, on the edge of the disreputable and impregnable labyrinth of the Tibbi Gali neighbourhood. Dirt and stench were permanent fixtures in this hangout for the scum of society. Mahmud was lord of Hira Mandi, Shahi Mohalla and Tibbi Gali, the three dance and prostitution neighbourhoods. He didn't go out much. The inhabitants were scared of him. He too followed Zulfikar Ali Bhutto's policies with interest. But he remained circumspect. He knew men too well to put his trust in a politician, especially one like Bhutto, motivated by the best intentions in the world. He had not welcomed the return of Asif Sahudiqi to the old city either. He was suspicious of all this hullabaloo for the son of a bourgeois who was establishing himself as a torch-bearer of the PPP to transform the lives of the poor. Since when did the rich care about the sufferings of the poor? And more importantly, why? Mahmud could sense that this greenhorn politician was going to upstage him. But he had the means to defend himself against anyone who encroached on his territory. A veritable army was at his beck and call. Ordinary men who could melt into any crowd, but were formidable when the need arose. These men were on the hunt for Shurma's attacker. Yet despite all their informants, it was not easy to dig out someone hiding in the shifty alleys of old Lahore. But it was also impossible to escape them forever. They were patient, stubborn and unrelenting, and they always found the one they were looking for.

It happened one evening. When they flushed out the young man, they killed him and threw his body into the Ravi on the other side of the ramparts.

10

Shanwaz was leaving Lahore for the first time in his life. He was going to Karachi in a vehicle hired for the occasion. He had dreamed of seeing his country for so long that he had refused to take the plane. Khalid Iqbal's landscapes were finally going to become a reality. Just the thought of it made him happy. But before the vast open spaces, he crossed Lahore's over-crowded suburbs. Without taking his eyes off the asphalt ribbon where the planet's subtlest and most orderly chaos reigned, he admired his chauffeur's incredible skill at weaving through the frenzied theatrical highway.

Sixty-six of his paintings had gone ahead to be exhibited at the Sheraton hotel in Karachi. Since the Alhamra fiasco, the gallery managers had been persuaded to create an event around Shanwaz's work, and they had invited the artist for the preview.

The road travelled along the banks of the Ravi before joining the Indus to the south. Some distance from the river, they crossed Multan, a torrid town which left Shanwaz with a memory of heat, dust, tombs and beggars. Soon the national highway left Punjab and entered the luxurious Sind province. They began an unending route across a region full of dacoits, elusive highwaymen who robbed motorists and slit the throats of villagers. They spent the night at Sukkur where their car ran into a camel convoy throwing up ochre dust into the medieval streets of the town. These images were engraved in Shanwaz's head like an enormous feast saturating his artist's imagination.

In the early morning, they crossed Sehwan-e-Sharif, on the day of Lala Shahbaz Qalandar's *Urs,* a religious festival commemorating the death of this Persian Sufi saint who had lived and died here. As the sun rose, the mud houses packed one against the other appeared even more surreal in the fog. Below, pilgrims, dancers and musicians milled about, barely visible in the shaded alleys... People had come from everywhere to pay a colourful homage to the Sufi saint. They stopped near his shrine where the crowd was all ecstasy and violence, chanting and praying to the sound of drums and cries. Shanwaz slipped inside and was greeted by an impressive carpet of humans extending all the way to the tomb, submerged in incense smoke and the lingering perfume of raining roses. Without daring to dislodge any of the pilgrims from their rapture, Shanwaz looked on, found his breath again, and was carried away for an instant to the brink of a profound mystery.

They rejoined the intensely busy road to Karachi again, passing out-of-control buses, and wide trucks slaloming between arrogant camels and prehistoric buffaloes harnessed to outlandish carts. Shanwaz thought he would die either of fright or of the sheer joy of seeing the unimaginable beauty of landscapes such as Lake Manchhar. On its peaceful turquoise waters, the boats of the Mohanas floated through the centuries with no desire to be attached to the banks of a world to which they quite clearly didn't belong. An old man told Shanwaz of the incredible legends that surrounded these peoples. They were of Dravidian origin, and had settled on the Indus long before the arrival of the Aryans in the eighteenth century B.C. The only disruption the Mohanas faced in their ancestral way of life was their forced conversion to Islam with the Arab invasion. The Arabs facilitated their passage from Hinduism to the Quran by flattering them with the title, 'Lords of the Indus'.

After a harassing day they arrived at the mouth of the delta, riding along the sacred banks of the old river where millenia-old lands struggled in vain against the foul black spirals that covered their stunning beauty in a mourning shroud. The Indus here took one last breath as it advanced through the countryside with its many branches, and expired with a spectacular final sigh at the threshold of the ravenous sea. They left the river and bifurcated to the west towards Karachi. Under the molten setting sun they passed the depressing misery of hellish neighbourhoods, and caught glimpses of the Dhobi Ghats, the world's largest laundry laid out as far as the eye could see along a dead tributary of the Indus. Shanwaz, incredulous and fascinated, watched the activity at 'Allah's laundry' where two thousand human robot beaters waded in the soapy muck twenty-four hours a day from the time they were children. They were untouchables in exile, come from India well before the Partition. Through the over-populated, grimy suburbs that were literally suffocating with the sand that the eastern winds carried from the Tharparkar desert, he understood that the life on this side with its sea of vehicles slowly crawling under an incandescent sun, was as unbearable as behind the walls of Lahore. All that remained of the little fishing port that was once Karachi were long desolate beaches behind which a dirty grey façade of cement had come up facing the sea. Shanwaz observed the vast murky sprawl that lost itself in an equally vast sky daubed in similar colours. He asked the driver to stop so he could stick his feet into this unknown substance that formed an ochre carpet for the rippling waves. He stood there facing the noisy, evil ocean, dizzy from staring at the infinite horizon. Nothing had ever captivated him so.

They continued down the unending tide of avenues. The city had no heart; it was a suffocating octopus with tentacles spreading everywhere to overcome the suffocation. In the hellish bumper-to-bumper traffic, Shanwaz had time to observe the nineteenth century Gothic Victorian buildings now rubbing shoulders with bastard constructions, sections of crumbling walls and opaque windows resolutely closed to the passage of time. He sensed that more than Lahore, there was a world surviving here behind the closed doors which refused any engagement with the outside world. In contrast, the streets were gregarious. People walked in them, and lived, pissed, and died in them without shame.

At the Sheraton, Shanwaz was welcomed with deference and quickly taken to his room. His first contact with luxury left him dumbstruck. All his life he had slept on nothing but a mattress on the floor with wrinkled, old bits of fabric for sheets, and here he could only marvel at the immaculate white sheets, the snug carpets, the thick linen drapes, the bathroom with a bathtub he could lie in, mirrors everywhere that reflected his already haggard face, the dark circles under his eyes, and the slightly thinning jet black hair. He felt so out of place in this ill-suited setting that he didn't dare sit on the bed or switch on the TV upon the chest, or even take his first bath. He stood by the window and observed the garden that lay at the foot of the hotel, while he went over the two days of travelling – the different landscapes now engraved in his head, the surprising towns he had crossed, and the extraordinary people he had met on the way. In the silent room, with only the hum of the air conditioner for company, he was already building other dreams under the waves of icy air chilling his bones. He felt a sudden desire to paint the beauty of the world, like Khalid Iqbal, the vast expanses of miraculous colours, the horizon where the sun lay dying. He wandered over the luminous body of this country that had revealed unimaginable secrets to him in just two days. He wanted to anchor his coarse hands in his country's earth. Realizing that he was shivering, he cursed the killer air conditioner, switched it off and decided to prepare himself for the preview.

The exhibition in-charge was waiting for him at the entrance to the vast hall overheated by the compact crowd of invitees jostling each other in front of the paintings. In one quick look Shanwaz knew that the hand-picked visitors were the elite of Karachi's rich and intelligentsia. The women's jewellery gleamed under the gallery walls and the men wore the distinguished outfit consisting of the very long black coat and tight white trousers sported by Jinnah, who had always had the reputation of a dandy. There was nothing of the feverish bonhomie of the Alhamra here. He found himself in a stiff, snobbish, self-centred society. Most had not come either for his talent or to buy any of his paintings. This posh gentry was here to be seen at an event in honour of a man who had caused an uproar.

Shanwaz would have liked the earth to swallow him up. This unfamiliar world was too much for him to take and he was seized by uncontrollable waves of shame. Gauche and miserable in his modest shalwar kameez, he probably resembled what he had always been – the son of a whore. An excruciating pain ripped through his body when the organiser took him by the arm to introduce him to meet important visitors. He had to pull himself together in an instant to avoid passing out, and he felt a pressing need to put an entire ocean between him and the others. But he was hemmed in by the crowds closing in, applauding as he went by, and his heaving lungs twisted his mouth into an unpleasant grimace. Women were smiling at him, men staring, and everywhere hands were extended towards him. Over the din, he could hear compliments, ludicrous questions and caustic remarks. The rest became a blur in his mind.

Although very few paintings were sold, the newspapers were elegiac in their praise. 'His realistic style matches the standards of contemporary art across the world today,' wrote the journalist for *The Star*, while *The Nation* introduced him as the heir of Pop Art. But Shanwaz knew nothing of Pop Art, or of Western painting. He had no arguments to justify his work. He would make up for this terrible ignorance once he was back in Lahore.

Once the work on his haveli was done, Asif Sahudiqi resumed his worldly life. There was no longer any call for lonely evenings in what now resembled a sumptuous Mughal palace. The inner courtyards with their marble fountains dotted with spotless doves, and the living rooms with crimson velvet sofas, were not made for emptiness. His friends, who had for long scorned the prohibited neighbourhoods of the old city, were surprised to see the splendour of the new residence. The air blossomed with sweet passion in this décor of surreal refinement, especially at night when the light from the candles danced on the surfaces of the thousands of mirrors dotting fabrics and drapes. Alcohol and drugs did the rounds of the sofas and cushions, served on engraved silver salvers carried by expressionless turbaned bearers. But for his friends, it was the presence of Hira Mandi's most beautiful dancers that amplified the delicious originality of these evenings. They were the only women capable of making Asif shiver with desire. Their perverse beauty worked like a diabolical elixir on him. Nazir, his man Friday, was in charge of recruitment. He belonged to the neighbourhood and knew Hira Mandi and its dancers well. He was a heartless tout and took handsome cuts from the money they were promised. He would discreetly bring them to the haveli in the night, and take them back at dawn with even greater precaution. Asif didn't want his political supporters to get wind of his nightly escapades.

As soon as he laid eyes on her, Aisha became his favourite dancer and official mistress. She captivated him at first sight. Her timidity effaced by experience, Aisha had become an artist of proven talent and flamboyant grace. Her black eyes mirrored her incredible sensuality. All the obscure passions and torpors of the East and the secret fatalism of Destiny could be seen in them. Asif observed her delicate instep with tireless fascination, while she furiously beat the floor with her heels, heels on which her billowing trousers fell just above her minuscule shoes, and the tiny bit of skin there that was so sensual in Aisha.

Shanwaz had no idea about his daughter's relationship with Asif. He was so caught up in his own life that he saw little of his family, and even less of Naseem and Aisha who came alive in the night. He left early in the morning to teach classes at the college and came back in the late afternoon to paint. But he *had* found the time to make Sana pregnant again – she would soon give birth to their fifth child. Now he hoped for a boy. After having given up Aisha to Naseem, to make up for the loss of Laila, it was out of the question that another of his daughters should enter the business. He was sending them to school, now that he had enough to pay for their studies. He regretted that he hadn't got it earlier – it would have pulled Naseem out of prostitution and avoided Aisha's entry into it.

After the Alhamra scandal, Asif invited Shanwaz to the haveli one evening, but he had refused, not willing to hobnob with someone he had no respect for. He was wary of him. Like his friend Mahmud Sahib, he had serious doubts about his honesty. But above all, although he would never admit it, Shanwaz was victim to pathological bashfulness in the presence of those who had money and power, in the presence of well-born people who rekindled the fire of shame that burned inside him. He was ill at ease in this milieu, out of his depth, and easily suffocated. Nothing helped, not money, not fame. Shame was written in his genes like a virus that could not be eliminated. It made him suffer terribly, like a defect that made him want to disappear without any explanations. He had never recovered from the insult he had suffered in his youth. It was a gaping, ignominious wound that pushed him into an abyss of humiliation. His honour as an honest man foundered and shattered to bits, and spoiled the slightest contact with the other, and his last ditch efforts seemed so pointless that he dreamed of disappearing like stardust. Sometimes he seemed to be weighed down by the burden of an essential sadness.

11

The 4th of April 1979 was a solemn day for the inhabitants of the old Mughal city. Zulfikar Ali Bhutto's reign ended before dawn on a noose in a Pakistani prison. People hadn't cried so much since the Partition. The mourning was tinged with revolt in the hearts of those who had believed in true freedom. Shanwaz, like the rest of Shahi Mohalla, feared the worst and bitterly regretted that Bhutto had floundered. The rise to power had been too much for him and he had embroiled himself in acts of violence that went as far as murder. As the reign of the 'democrat' disintegrated, one man watched from the shadows and patiently waited for his time to come. The assassination of a close aide of the prime minister was a well-timed affair. In 1977, General Zia-ul-Haq had the army behind him and was ready to impose martial law. He had Bhutto arrested, but was forced to release him for lack of proof. When the deposed prime minister came back from jail to Lahore, three million people had come out to welcome him with cries of 'Jiye Bhutto! Long live Bhutto!'

Shanwaz had joined the jubilation on the Mall, close to the National College of Art. Surrounded by his students, which included excited young girls from good families, he had hailed the liberation of the messiah, hoping he would soon take up the reins of power again and get rid of Zia. But nothing of the sort happened. The General, taken aback by Bhutto's popularity, hastened to throw him into prison again and took retaliatory measures. Soldiers were given orders to flog anyone saying 'Long live Bhutto' or 'Long live democracy'. Public punishments increased with an eye to setting examples. The country was faced with a savageness that obliged people to lie low.

In Lahore, men set themselves on fire to protest against the death penalty accorded to their Prime Minister. Shanwaz scanned the front page of the PPP's newspaper, *Musawaat*, for a familiar face amongst the pictures of the miserable martyrs. After Bhutto's arrest, the newspaper had increased its circulation to over a hundred thousand copies in Lahore itself. But the printing press could not keep up with the demand and the more enterprising souls sold the papers at a higher rate in the market. It was worth ten rupees in the black market. More than what the average Pakistani earned in a day. Zia had the press seized and the offices shut down, and in the same breath, ordered complete censorship of the media. Any journalist who broke the law was punishable by whipping and twenty-five years in prison. Then, after Bhutto's execution, he prohibited all political parties. Under Ayub Khan, the army had represented the ultimate guarantee for the internal security of the country and its territorial integrity. Zia went a step further and the army became the primary driving force behind the ideological state and the imposition of Islam as the intrinsic core of political life.

No one in the old city missed the general's first speech on television – 'Pakistan, which was created in the name of Islam, will continue to survive only if it sticks to Islam. If you take Islam out of Pakistan, it will collapse like a house of cards. It will have no reason to survive,' he concluded, leaving the inhabitants speechless and on the edge of a precipice. They all understood that he actually meant the establishment of the *sharia* and its system of Quranic punishments – amputations, whipping and stoning. Women would be veiled and cloistered, and men would have the right to have four wives whom they could use and throw out as it pleased them. This barbaric wave of regressive laws plunged the country in uncertainty and reinforced the tyrannical rule.

In January 1978, in pursuit of his Islamic utopia, Zia ordered his first massacre as soon as he came into power. Labourers in Multan's textile factory, who were on strike because the owners had reduced their bonuses, had decided to demonstrate to express their discontent. They never got the chance. Three days before the planned date, the army locked the factory gates, took position on the roof and shot at the crowd, killing hundreds of trapped workers. It was one of the worst massacres in the country's history. This was Zia's warning to the members of the working classes, the backbone of the PPP, to give in or die. Lahore's inhabitants were in shock on hearing the news. The PPP's offices were closed down. Even Asif Sahudiqi didn't dare intercede. He had the flags and Bhutto's portraits removed from his offices in front of the Barood Khana. The reign of terror was here to stay for long.

In Shahi Mohalla, Mahmud Sahib held a veritable war council. Secret meetings and coalitions were necessary for quiet but effective resistance. To keep up a united front, he decided to enter into politics and introduced himself to the authorities as the councillor for the neighbourhood's security, the only way to reach a compromise on the recent intolerance of the powers. One day, during a councillors' conference, a general came in with orders to close Hira Mandi to dancers. Mahmud Sahib addressed the general, 'You cannot close this neighbourhood without taking into account the future of our women. If you take away their livelihood, you need to help them find another place in society. Those of you present here ready to marry a prostitute raise your hands.'

Not one hand went up.

'As long as you don't marry their daughters and give your daughters to their sons, society will never evolve,' Mahmud Sahib ranted mercilessly.

The order was revoked. Hira Mandi was not closed. The prudish Islamists didn't dare cross the obligatory opaque cotton curtains that now hung in the doorways of the small salons. But in February, the Mullahs prohibited the Basant festival, uncaring of the disappointed children who waited every year for this extraordinary jubilation, just as children in the west wait for Father Christmas. There was a formal prohibition on flying pigeons and kites. The pigeons because they symbolized the souls of Sufi saints and protected their mausoleums. The kites because flying them from the roofs invaded women's privacy. So, on Basant, in response to these laughable measures, the inhabitants collected on the roofs and sent hundreds of fire crackers into the air. Shanwaz took his three youngest girls, Rubi, Rami and Naika, up to the terrace on the roof. They shared a few rare moments together. The girls, happy to have him there, showered him with their affection, and cuddled, kissed and hugged him. He was moved by the affection that his usual aloofness didn't encourage, and he basked in their loving looks, their arms around him, and admired the little lights that bloomed just above the full moon, lighting up the night in magical colours.

When Ramadan approached, Zia encouraged the religious fundamentalists to crack down on those who allowed themselves concessions with regard to Quranic texts. Fasting during the holy month had always been a matter of personal choice for Pakistan's Muslims. Under the tyrant's reign, restaurants and grocery shops had to remain closed from dawn to dusk. Water supplies were cut in universities and even in the bathrooms to prevent anybody from drinking. It was like the Inquisition, with fundamentalists prowling the streets, knocking on doors in the middle of the night to make sure people were preparing the *sehri,* the traditional meal eaten before dawn. Drinking, eating or smoking in public were enough to be arrested. In Pakistan, all that remained was the brutality of a supposedly religious regime.

One morning, on arriving at his college, Shanwaz was stopped from going in by a guard whom he knew well. The man was all apologies, and very embarrassed to have to do his superiors' dirty work. The new administration had fired Shanwaz on the grounds that his subject was offensive to the principles of Islam. Human representation was prohibited by the Quran, and he no longer had the right to give subversive classes to young students. He had been thrown out without any compensation and suddenly found himself without a job.

He went back home profoundly disheartened. The persecutions were not going to stop there. Already disapproved of as an artist under Bhutto, he would be despised by all the mullahs. He was not just losing his job, but also the renown that he had worked so hard to achieve. No one would exhibit his works any longer. No one would risk buying his work. And the little money he had made with the sale of his paintings was not going to take him very far. If he had been alone, it wouldn't have been so dramatic, he didn't need much to live on. But his family was used to a comfortable life, his daughters went to a well-known, expensive school – he couldn't suddenly withdraw them from there. As usual, he found himself facing an abyss of loneliness. The only person he could think of confiding in was his mother. But the almost sixty-year-old Naseem, who had been unmoved by her son's short-lived fame, was like a lost soul, her life bearable only because of the strange consolation of having Aisha. She was indifferent to everything else. She would lie all day on the comfortable mattress of rupees that she guarded like a treasure trove under a worm-eaten plank in her room. She had cleverly negotiated Aisha's exclusivity with Nazir, Asif Sahudiqi's right-hand man. Her business prowess had gotten the better of the sickly-thin, lanky recruiter's greed, his little black moustache like a line across his upper lip accentuating his sinister frame.

Aisha was at the height of her splendour. Her renown went beyond the walls of Lahore. For her, Asif received Ustad Fateh Ali Khan, one of the most phenomenal singers of the times, in his haveli. The Ustad belonged to an illustrious family of Qawwali singers whose lineage could be traced to the fourteenth century. He was accompanied by his musicians, all members of his family. In Qawwali, a form of Sufi devotional songs, repetition leads to a sort of trance and ecstasy. By his side, the Ustad's son, Nusrat raised his heavenly voice to the stars. His voice was like the echo of a forgotten memory, a piece of clear sky blowing in the wind, a voice with infinite modulation that would earn him the title of Shahenshah-e-Qawwali, Qawwali's brightest star. After the dance, Aisha sat by Asif's side, proud to be the one adored by the man wanted by all the women. They sank into the cushions and smoked and drank until their desire was too much to handle, and they had to leave. Under the starry skies, the Qawwali continued to envelope the night in divine delight.

Shanwaz had renounced his relationship with his daughter for so many years that he did not care much about what she was up to. He had removed this part of himself like an amputated limb. He avoided crossing her path, which wasn't always easy living just a floor away. He knew that she was one of Hira Mandi's most cherished dancers, but he refused to make her portrait. Why inflict such torture on himself? There was a rumour that a film producer was interested in her – every dancer's dream come true. Becoming an actress was the icing on the cake. In these films copied from their Indian counterparts, the directors established the pedigree of the sophisticated and elegant Mughal courtesans, and portrayed a highly glamorous image of the prostitute. Aisha was the perfect woman for a role like this. But Naseem, the only one who would decide, was hesitant. If Aisha left Shahi Mohalla, would she come back one day? Fame and fortune would be hers – would she not then forget her past and vehemently deny her origins, as all the others did when they became stars? Aisha would soon be twenty, an age to make children. A star's life was short and producers didn't even wait for the first wrinkle before rejecting a woman for being too old and replacing her with younger, more enticing girls. Naseem was deeply attached to the traditions of Shahi Mohalla. Too many dancers went to pieces in abject misery because they didn't have daughters. Too many of them ended up in Tibbi galli, the sordid neighbourhood just behind Hira Mandi, where the sons of these poor dancers found an outlet for their lazy decline by becoming their pimps. Naseem remembered how Tibbi Galli had once been the street for cheaper prostitutes at ten rupees a fuck.

The girls were managed by a Pathan from Peshawar in the west. It was their neighbourhood. They filled it with the girls they lured from the countryside with false promises of marriage, and threw into the flesh trade once they reached Lahore. The girls spent the rest of their lives there with no means of escaping their destiny. From morning until night they sat waiting for clients on a chair in the street in front of a minuscule room with only a bed inside. They were not allowed to get pregnant, so as not to affect their profitability. If it did happen, they went for an abortion before their pimps could find out, to a shrew who took her risks on them. Some died of it. But, slowly the Pathans became less welcome in the neighbourhood and it turned into a shelter for old prostitutes. There was something brutal about Tibbi Gali. It reeked of the violence of extreme poverty with houses as derelict as its hideously dolled-up human wrecks, perched on the edges of staircases in serpentine alleys so narrow it was difficult for two people to pass, and lined on each side by gutters where men squatted to piss before going in to fuck. Life in these squalid, dark, humid and dirty places was even fouler than in the rest of the city.

Naseem sometimes made short trips there to take some clothes to Shurma's mother, her cousin. Since Shanwaz had decided to send the young disfigured Shurma into a plastic surgery clinic, he had deprived her mother of her sole breadwinner. The man she took care of had compensated for the deprivation by setting her up in Tibbi Gali. To get there, Naseem had to cross Novelty Chowk, the transvestite neighbourhood, locally known as Unix. Signs above the street already gave an idea of what was to come. Each day brought its share of tragedies for these extremely fragile beings, mocked and avoided like the plague. During the day only the older ones came out, bent over their walking sticks, with bristly red hair and glazed eyes, their wizened skin always covered in pink powder, and cracked lips where a few lines of red persisted. The derelict wrecks seemed even more pathetic in their absolute need to please in exchange for a little human warmth.

There was a little passage that led from Novelty Chowk to Tibbi Gali, known only to the locals. Naseem was never at ease in the midst of this hangout for beggars, cripples and other dregs of humanity. Violence rent the electric air. That day, in the very first alley, an enormous woman sat cross-legged in the middle of a wooden bed, blocking her way, and smiling at her pleasantly. A sort of poultice in a disgusting bird-shit-green was smeared all over her hair, making her already misshapen face with its mass of wrinkled fat look like something made of mud. Another, dressed in a filthy shalwar kameez stood in the doorway. A hint of a beard showed through her made-up face. Inside, it was a holy mess, a jumble of filth and old furniture suggestive of the apathy into which the human with no future falls. On a chair nearby, a young pimp with a mass of henna-dyed hair and the sinister air of an old drag queen sat picking his teeth. In this sewer-like humidity, these women in flowery cotton shalwar kameezes in a single file on either side of the street had only a few square metres to live in. The luckiest stayed above the stench, on a little wrought-iron balcony, with a parrot in a cage for company. Further down, a woman of indeterminate age sat motionless on one of the three steps of her doorway, her hands folded on her massive stomach. Behind the gaudy white, red and blue mask, her face reflected her acute awareness of the absurdity of it all. Naseem could not see the once fine and delicate lines of her cousin's face. Her large kohl-laden eyes were lost under the withered, outrageously coloured eyelids. Naseem knew just what she had escaped.

The two women entered the single room. Naseem placed the clothes on the floor and listened to her cousin rant about Shanwaz whom she blamed for her plight. Naseem agreed. She too blamed her son for meddling in affairs that were none of his concern. Even worse, he had broken with the sacrosanct rule of each one for himself. To each his misery, thought Naseem. Which was why she felt she was a little to blame and tried to make up with her rare visits. Besides, she couldn't just forget their youth, the memories of happy days that they evoked to warm their hearts. Of course, Naseem had nothing to complain about. She was in a far better position than her cousin. She lacked nothing. Except love. So, in fact, the essential. Jaffer, the only love of her life had stopped coming to see her. He had become weak from illness and remained holed up in his house until death took him to Allah's paradise.

When she lingered on for too long, two pimps in white came to take an angry look at the stranger distracting their game. Naseem left by other convoluted alleys that turned full circles and formed invisible cells that seemed impossible to escape. In fact, nobody ever did get out of Tibbi Gali. Sometimes, Naseem would see an eye looking out from behind the tiny windows, prostitutes who had reached the age where it was no longer possible to market their wares in public. They had nothing more to offer than a dry opening like dead wood that they would coat with grease. These poor old women were left for the most down-and-out customers who slinked slyly into the dark room where she was already lying on the bed, her shirt rolled up to her face, trousers lowered and legs spread wide enough for the client to do what he needed without any delay. It lasted just long enough for her nostrils to be assailed by the wretched stink of poverty that went hand in hand with the miasma and stench of the flesh. The man would throw a miserable rupee on the floor or sneak away like a thief of depravity.

Prostitutes in Pakistan had always had a place in the lives of the bourgeoisie and the politicians, but Zia, who had embarked upon the Islamization of the country by sending his commandos everywhere to beat and punish miscreants, ordered that Tibbi Gali be shut down.

Naseem heard what happened from a terrorized transvestite who had watched from his window the brutality with which the police had dragged the women to prison after beating and whipping them in the streets. Zia, unable to transform his personal faith into a state system, decided on a tyrannical rule where nobody was safe. Since then, all that was left in Tibbi Gali was a handful of miserable, dying whores who had lost everything. After this police crackdown, nobody ever heard of

Shurma's mother again. Even Naseem didn't try to find out what happened to her.

She was sitting cross-legged on the frayed satin bed cover, deep in thought, when Shanwaz entered her room. She raised her head only after a long moment. The décor hadn't changed in the past forty years, but the strawberry pink she had so liked had faded and the furniture was collapsing with age. She was surprised to see her son. And he was suddenly intimidated. His head filled with images. He saw himself as a child again, crawling towards the perfectly orderly and clean room whose heady perfume filled the air and nauseated him. A tub filled with water in a corner, with a towel next to it. He could see himself alone in the middle of this world full of mysteries that haunted his nights and that he had no access to. Yet he felt a peculiar pleasure in finding himself in the midst of his mother's most private life. The secrets had been revealed with time. What remained of the mother he had so loved and so feared was this woman with the dull, hard eyes slouching into her ignominy, her hair scant and greying, her body and skin ravaged and wrinkled, the once proud, fine, willowy silhouette now an ill-defined mass.

She stared at him in silence. He didn't dare raise his eyes towards her, uneasy, ready to burst into tears, not from despair but from sadness, like when he was five and Naseem would give him a hurried hug and leave, abandoning her devastated boy to his strange sorrow. Mother and son hadn't spoken much in a long time. Both went about their business on their own. In Shahi Mohalla, the essential thing was to survive. And for some years neither had had anything to complain about. Money was coming in. But when she saw his face, she understood that life was taking its toll on his happiness. She too was worried about the political upheavals and their impact on their daily lives. The constant police presence in the evenings scared the girls. Just last week, three policemen armed with sticks had arrived in the bazaar and had mercilessly set upon the women, accusing them of wanting to invite men upstairs with them. Shanwaz had depicted this episode of pure brutality in a giant painting which he wanted to show off one day as proof of the absurdity of his country's history. To avoid problems, many clients came to pick up girls and took them outside the walls, to tacky hotels, forcing them to drink alcohol and making them dance to music from Indian films. At dawn, the girls were perniciously raped and abandoned on the streets with just enough to take a rickshaw back home. They couldn't even complain, knowing full well that any judge would turn the situation on its head and accuse them of being responsible for the risks they took by being out alone at night. Men, knowing they would go scot-free no matter what they did, became increasingly violent and used the poor girls to vent their frustrations.

For Shanwaz, Pakistan hadn't stopped paying for the savage tragedy of its creation. When he was ten years old, he had seen thousands of people kill each other because of one man's dream. Since then, Jinnah's dream of a pure Islamic republic had degenerated and led to a bigoted, narrow-minded society of uneducated men religiously indulging in debauchery. Shanwaz now had much reason to fear the fundamentalists who filled the Badshahi. They prayed in ecstasy for a Pakistan that would return to the era of the Prophet, and their vision of this new state had no place for miscreants like Shanwaz. It remained as foggy as the reason that had led to the creation of their country, but their fanaticism went beyond all reasoning.

Shanwaz was aware of the danger he represented to himself and his family. He would have liked to talk to his mother about his anguish, his fears, and his loneliness. But in her old age, Naseem had become resolutely, almost neurotically, self-centred. All that mattered to her was Aisha, her only source of income, while the others – Sana had just given birth to a fifth – slept peacefully on the floor above without earning a rupee for her. She resented her son's obstinacy in not putting them into the business, whiling away their time like their good-for-nothing mother, whereas any other Hira Mandi dancer would have blessed the skies for such an exceptional gift of five daughters. She cursed this self-centred son who cared only for his paintings and neglected the potential source of income for his so-called progressive ideas. She raged inwardly at the idea of her cousin living in Tibbi Gali because of his irresponsible generosity. What was the use of spending a fortune on a girl whose life was wasted anyway, since she could never get her face back? She had kept it all bottled up for so long that she was quite pleased to see him standing on the threshold of her room. If he dared show his face, it meant he needed her. She was determined not to give in. That was the last day they ever exchanged any words.

12

One morning in 1981, Shanwaz came across an article in *The Nation* that talked about the English Prime Minister Margaret Thatcher's visit to Afghan refugee camps in Peshawar. The 'Iron Lady' referred to Zia ul-Haq as 'the last bastion of the free world'. It made Shanwaz balk. The term couldn't have been more distasteful to the Pakistani people, after four years of subjugation under the merciless dictator. The war in Afghanistan hadn't helped. The country had become a puppet in the hands of the United States. The military in power had no idea what to do with all the arms that the Americans were plying them with, or with the tonnes of drugs coming from Afghanistan that had elevated Pakistan to the rank of no.1 heroin supplier in the world. And a select band of the 'faithful' filled their coffers with millions of dollars, while Zia's regime looked the other way, content to take its share.

Each day brought its share of bad news. Headlines were enough to give an idea of the catastrophic state the country was in. 'Massacres between Sunnis and Shi'as in Karachi'. Zia's regime played up communal hatred. 'Fifty thousand Sufis from Sind block the national highway for several days'. Those who stood for humanism and democracy did not accept this form of Islam. 'Hudood ordinance shocks women'. Khomeini was back in power in Iran, and Zia had adopted his infamous ordinance, that perverted, barbaric judicial system that laid all the blame for rape and adultery on women. But despite all this, the Reagan administration continued to support Zia who had allied himself with the Saudi Arabian fundamentalists of the *Jammat-e-Islami*, reputed for their complete intolerance. This Islamization policy had dreadful consequences for the Hindu, Parsi and Shi'a minorities.

The Pakistan of the Partition era seemed almost like a liberal utopia compared to the current plague of religious fanaticism. Shanwaz remembered old newspaper photographs of Jinnah giving prizes to women athletes in shorts. Lahore was then knows as the 'Paris of the East' due to the numerous cabarets that lined the Mall. Every decade that followed had further eroded the progressive spirit of the sub-continent's Muslims. The dictator general had forever sealed the coffin of tolerance. And in Shanwaz's eyes, Zia's generation was a mutating species of individuals with perverted, confused minds, who had nothing else to offer but hypocrisy to reconcile their mystical beliefs with contemporary realities. Over the years, corruption had eaten away at the state – an unstoppable merry-go-round of public religion and private pillaging.

Shut away in his workshop where he spent most of his days in a bizarre, dismal atmosphere, Shanwaz had seen his paintings come back one by one. The few galleries exhibiting them had very quickly withdrawn their support, fearing trouble. The canvasses were piled high everywhere, and he didn't have any space to work anymore. He decided to clean up the ground floor of the house. The two big rooms had always served as a junkyard for the other floors. They were full of piles of decrepit furniture, old cartons, worn clothes and broken toys. A world of junk that was taken away by rag pickers in a dilapidated cart pulled by a skinny donkey, men in foul tatters who, like a greedy army of ants, were ready to pick up anything. The two empty rooms now showed off their antique Mughal architecture – sculpted wooden beams, Gothic arches, stucco niches, all in an advanced state of disrepair due to the work of rot and vermin. Even the gorgeous tiled floor had disappeared under the grime. Shanwaz paid Taraq, a young Christian neighbour, to clean, scrub, polish and repaint the whole place garnet red, a colour that would stand out in the artificial light of the lamps.

In the neighbourhood, Christians were even worse off than the Muslims. Taraq shared a single room with the seven members of his family – his ageing parents, his wife and their four children. They stole a few intimate moments at night when everyone was asleep, making love in less than five minutes, or sometimes they would hide in a dark corner of the courtyard to fornicate like hunted animals. Shanwaz gave him work whenever he could, the poor boy had to feed his entire family on his own and pay exorbitant rent for the hovel they called home. While Taraq spruced up the ground floor, Shanwaz scoured the old city looking for old Mughal doors and delicately sculpted wooden mashrabiahs to give it soul. In some streets, the houses abandoned by their owners were a heap of rubble that nobody cared much for, since the inhabitants had no idea of the worth of all that they had left behind to rot. Not many had adopted Asif Sahudiqi's example of protecting and preserving their heritage.

In a few weeks, the two rooms were unrecognizable. Shanwaz hung the paintings on the freshly painted walls, and the place took on the airs of an art gallery. He was very proud of how his paintings blended with a sculpture of a Hindu god found in the remains of a haveli. The odours of incense exuded by the solemn, magnificently hieratic statue mingled with the gold powder of the daylight that filtered through the minuscule openings of the mashrabiahs. To fill up the empty space, he placed a few tables and chairs around for possible guests – he imagined a sort of welcoming living room where he could have tea and a chat with friends. In the East, it was unimaginable to receive guests without offering them some sort of sustenance, so he set up a little niche where drinks and food could be prepared, and put Taraq in charge so he could make some money from tips. He suspended a sign in front of the house with the name of his latest creation written in Islamic green: *Kunda*. The word denoted the ritual cuisine prepared by Shi'as during religious ceremonies. This salon revived a dream of well-being, of comfort, and peace that he was unable to find, and had never found in his own home. Sana hated his paintings and refused to have any of his drawings in the apartment on the last floor where she continued to make him and his daughters live in a coarse, gloomy pigsty in which the television blared all day long.

Visitors were slow to come in the beginning, and the curious barely dared poke their heads in before they fled as though they'd seen the devil. But soon, the incredible spell of the place held back the more adventurous souls – its unusual coloured walls lit by little orangey lamps that warmed the intimate ambiance created by the imperious women piercing the souls of passers-by from their high perches. More and more of them came. Shanwaz liked to go across the room when it was full. He savoured the scene in the sweltering heat of the gallery cooled by a single fan. He listened to the conversations with half an ear, observing the personality of the seated guests, mostly well-to-do people, mostly educated youth and women who always came with a husband, a brother or an uncle. On Fridays, families hanging around in the Badshahi's gardens, made the effort to come to his door and sit with their children, facing the many taboos hanging from the walls.

Kunda made a name for itself amongst a sophisticated crowd of people who were happy to discover such an unusual tea house in Lahore. But it also made a name for itself amongst the mullahs who had become Zia's weapons for Islamization. The *fatwa*, a judgement on good and evil dictated by these 'men of God', took on a fearful meaning for Shanwaz, the damned, blasphemous painter. First, as a warning, they broke the signboard and left it on the ground in pieces. Another day, two bearded men nabbed him in front of his house, their hard eyes boring into his. Shanwaz didn't blink an eyelid. The threat was more explicit. They advised him to close down his evil den. Shanwaz turned on his heel without a word and entered the gallery. He would never give in to the demands of religious extremists. He made an even bigger and clearer sign, which disappeared one day, with everything else, in the macabre dancing flames.

During all these years of the dictatorship, the PPP became the only voice of salvation and hope for many Pakistanis. Zulfikar Ali Bhutto's daughter had come back from her exile in Great Britain, and taken up the reins of her father's party to make herself heard in the ravaged country. Benazir arrived in Lahore on 9 April 1986. In the city, celebrations had started the day before. Everywhere people danced and sang to the rhythm of drums, drank and ate in the streets for free. PPP flags hung from balconies and street lamps. Even fundamentalists from the *Jamaat-e-Islami* sold flags and pictures of Benazir, rejecting their higher principles to take advantage of this opportunity to make a fast buck. The entire city was in the hands of a people who had forgotten the failures of Bhutto senior, the massacres of the final phases, the blood that was shed due to the monumental errors of a crazed, fanatical utopian. The charisma and magic of the name itself was enough for the most wronged. Students drove around the city in Suzuki trucks singing songs in punjabi. '*Aaj te ho gai Bhutto, Bhutto*' 'today, there is none but Bhutto'. The crowds came in cars, in buses, in bullock carts, in trucks, on foot.

It was the first time after many long years of horror and repression that there was such jubilation again. Nobody slept that night. Cries, songs and prayers filled the air. An old man with tears in his eyes hung on to Shanwaz for a moment and walked with him. An old woman joined them, half-crying, half-laughing, and caught his other arm. Shanwaz was as moved as these old people who, after the sufferings of the Partition, had lived on one lost hope after another, and he drowned his feelings in the heat of the humid shadows. Stuck in the midst of the crowd he felt his lungs give way to asthmatic anxiety but a sudden gust of air revived him and pulled him out of the suffocating atmosphere around him. There had been no official mourning after Bhutto's hanging. Repression had forbidden any demonstration of revolt or distress. Ten years later, people were finally giving vent to their sorrow, as much as they celebrated the return of Benazir, the former prime minister's dearest daughter. It was an extraordinary night of jubilation for Shanwaz, as though God and his prophets had announced the arrival of a new dawn for the world.

The authorities had placed heavy metal barriers and barbed wire barricades to contain the crowds around the airport where Benazir's plane was to land. But joy was mixed with fear. A million human beings formed a sweaty, sticky sea along the streets, packed into balconies and on rooftops, hanging out of trees and on lamp posts.

On the morning of the 10th of April, it took ten hours for Benazir's convoy to reach the centre of Lahore. Meanwhile, the crowd had swelled from one million to three. Hundreds of coloured balloons filled the air. Benazir's jeep was covered in rose petals. To the Pakistanis, the young thirty-five year old woman looked like a fairy from the Indus, tall and slim, all dressed in white, with a thin white cotton dupatta covering her thick black hair. An imposing Benazir greeted the delirious people, waving gracefully and smiling from her perch in her slow-moving vehicle. The black, green and red of the PPP seemed to be the only colours that day in Lahore. The flags and banners of the party formed an unending billowing arch in the warm air. Donkeys and buffaloes had the colours of the PPP braided into their manes and tails. The jubilation had reached frenetic heights.

Benazir gave a speech in Iqbal Park, facing the Badshahi burning under the last rays of the sun, and also facing the Lahore fort where so many political prisoners had been tortured and killed by Zia's men. Like her father twenty-five years ago, she too pledged to sacrifice everything to ensure the rights of the people while her supporters shouted, 'Out with Zia!'

But Zia's forces took their revenge four months later. On the 14th of August, Pakistan's Independence Day, the army shot at PPP supporters in Lahore, and everywhere else in the country. Hundreds died and thousands were wounded. Shanwaz turned forty-nine that day. But it completely slipped his mind.

13

Surayya's son had fallen asleep on the yellow floral bedcover under the cold neon light. Her daughter, in little pigtails, sat next to the rickety doors of the wooden cupboards, playing with ping pong racquets with cloth balls stuck to them. The television was blaring. Some stupid Pakistani soap with a gaudily made up actress whose thickly outlined mouth shone like chocolate ice cream, and whose cheeks were streaked with fake tears. Cartoon-like expressions, melodramatic actors decked out in garish costumes for a cheap western look. On the screen, two lovers were fighting, arguing. Surayya had picked up a bag to throw at Shanwaz. Both were sitting cross-legged on the floor on the worn carpet, shouting at each other, and fiction and reality seemed to become one. She laughed and she cried like the painted heroine with fake tears, but she was really crying, and her heavy body shook with her sobs. She looked haggard with her earthy skin devoid of make up, in a red shalwar kameez under which she hid her layers of fat. Nothing pleased her more than when he told her convincingly that she was getting back her hourglass figure, that she had become incredibly slimmer in a few days. She smiled. His eyes calmed her. He could take her hand and she didn't slap his face. Her eyes looked at him gently, lovingly almost. He was going away. He promised to come back in two days. Yes, he would stay the entire evening with her. She believed him and let him leave with a smile full of anxiety and tenderness. The neighbour's socks were drying on the balustrade, and on the corridor balcony was the underwear of the family on the first floor. Through the open door he could see the old mother, one foot in the grave, sitting unstably on a bed with her eyes closed. The children were on the floor, finishing their dinner.

Her watery green eyes fell on him like a delinquent wave in an ocean ready to engulf him. He thought he would melt and disappear under her forceful gaze with its fragile remains of suffering. An intense heat filled his mind and he couldn't think any more. His body was overcome with adrenaline and a fierce desire. The brush trembled in his limp fingers. His throat was choked, and he wasn't sure if he was alive any longer, faced with this angelic creature who was making him giddy. She lay on an old sofa, wearing her most precious ornaments – a diamond nose-pin to accentuate the lines of her nose, and on her jet black hair a tiara whose rubies fell like drops of blood on her dark skin. Silver earrings rang in her ears and her arms were covered from the wrists to the elbows in glass bangles held by silk ribbons. The multicoloured rings emphasised her delicate wrists. He was gripped with a burning emotion that rose from the depths of his past like a fire finally freed after years of lying dormant. He went weak in the knees as the heat travelled down his back.

This was how Shanwaz fell for Surayya, a Hira Mandi dancer whose animal sensuality was already on the wane. His last mooring.

At seven, Surayya danced and sang with the grace and sensuality of a Mughal goddess. She had just turned twelve when she had her ring ceremony and was sold for one night to a prince from Saudi Arabia who paid a colossal sum for the privilege of deflowering her. She had only a vague memory of that night, she had been drugged by the man so he could get the most out of her. Her radiant beauty soon made her a sought-after dancer. Surayya loved her profession – she was inebriated with fame, her admirers and money. Seduction was a pleasure, a reason to live. But the ravages of alcohol and drugs had already begun to show when her family saved her from disaster and married her off to a rich Pakistani who paid a fortune to marry her. In Shahi Mohalla, the clan accepted the departure of a woman if a dowry of several million rupees was paid to compensate for the missing breadwinner.

Her husband gave her four children before taking her to Dubai where she transformed herself into the perfect wife, mother and mistress of the house. A symbol of virtue who so bored her husband that he decided to find passion and miracles elsewhere. She decided to take a lover to spite him, forgetting that she was risking a husband's vengeance. The humiliated man denounced her to the police. She risked the death penalty in an Islamic country. She was thrown into prison with her two daughters, and managed to escape with the help of a friend who paid generous bribes. The husband had meanwhile regained his composure and agreed to let her leave for Lahore with the girls. But there was no question of taking the boys, she would never see them again.

On her return to Shahi Mohalla, she was no longer young enough to be a dancer, but her womanly maturity was still attractive to the clients she received in her house. She had fallen in love with a rich Lahori dealer and had kept the child she believed was his, but hadn't succeeded in keeping him. Abandoned and miserable, she had returned to drugs for solace and had two more children with a neighbour who had married her. But the idyll hadn't lasted long – her jealous husband beat her and mistreated her and she spent her time trying to save the two children he wanted to take away from her. She had forgotten that in Hira Mandi you didn't fall in love with someone from the neighbourhood. It killed the 'business'. Her tumultuous love affairs and successive pregnancies had driven her clients away.

Surayya decided it was time to act. In a newspaper one day she saw the portraits of Hira Mandi dancers but she had never met this painter that everyone was talking about. She dreamed of being one of his models on a painting exhibited somewhere. Her eyes lit up for him in the grimy light of the workshop, and her soul came alive again. Surayya lived just one street away from Shanwaz with her two youngest children. At first she was taken aback by how much she fascinated him, then the artist's crazed look of desire for her lifted the veils of fog that had been shrouding her life. After so many nights of anguish, her entire body opened up like a flower in the first dew of dawn.

No woman had so enthralled Shanwaz since Laila. After the workshop, they met in the room where the children played in front of the TV. Surayya made them leave despite their protests and locked them in the room that housed the kitchen. Then she and Shanwaz locked themselves in her room, and began their seduction with whisky, languorous stares and furtive touches. She was sensuality itself, a woman born to beguile men, to captivate and engulf them in endless pleasure. She turned on the fan to air the stuffy room. Her hand held on tightly to a little bag that seemed to hold innumerable treasures. She pulled a stereo out from under the bed and slipped a cassette in. Shanwaz was half-lying on the floral bedcover, his body brimming with a desire he hadn't felt in a very long time. When the music burst out from the little speaker, she stood up, her arms flew out like wings pulled by the wind, the fingers bent outwards moving with the grace of a swan. Her head moved from side to side, her long, black undone hair wrapped itself around her body, while her feet tapped the floor in a furious rhythm. Above the din made by the fan and the high-pitched modulation of the music, the voice that began singing moved Shanwaz to the depths of his soul. A deep, warm voice, bewitching, magnetic, full of despair and clarity that would enchant him forever.

For Shanwaz a woman's love showed through in her jealous tantrums. With Surayya, he got it all. She attacked him all the time, reproached him for a thousand things, didn't like other dancers being his models, and was jealous of Sana despite the indifference he had always felt for his wife. She wouldn't believe him, convinced that she was a real rival. She could not imagine her ugly and stupid as Shanwaz described her. How was it possible that a man like him had accepted such a sorry marriage? But what motivated Surayya's sometimes ferocious jealousy was not so much her love for Shanwaz as a profound unease that had deepened with the wounds of her tumultuous years.

At thirty-five, she weighed ninety-five kilos from drinking to forget her despair and to have something to offer to the clients who still climbed up the two floors. It was an infernal merry-go-round in which she consumed more alcohol and drugs to forget her physique, and was trapped in her own spiralling loneliness.

She only rarely saw her mother, because their meetings systematically ended in a spat. In fact, it was quite simple, she had spats with everybody, because everybody was indifferent and miserable. She lived in the constant fear of being beaten, the horror of growing old, the pain of having lost her children, the terror of being abandoned. She missed her oldest girl, Hina, a fifteen-year old beauty who had left for a career in Dubai to cater to her mother's needs. Her sleep was tormented by nightmares since Hina disappeared.

She would then run her seductive hand through her dishevelled hair. Desire was palpable in her husky voice heavy with whisky and nicotine as she softly sang old poetic songs 'It's the voice of whisky,' she would say, bursting into peals of mocking laughter. Her last hopes were on Alina, the last little one who was already very glamorous for a five-year old. She was counting on her to build her a house for her old age. At twelve, Alina would be a dancer. But not one of those to be found in the backs of the shops on Hira Mandi's streets. With the advent of mobile phones, the girls could now make up a network of clients of a certain social status without needing to be on the streets. That was reserved for the small fry, the rabble. Her beauty would perhaps attract film producers. Society's disdain for girls from this milieu didn't leave them much choice, and things were getting worse with time and the fundamentalists. Often, scared of the police, they would look for a pimp's protection because it had become too dangerous to work and their livelihoods were so threatened.

Shanwaz couldn't paint her enough. Her Rubens-like shape inspired and excited him. He made her bigger, unable to understand how he who had been repulsed by the overlapping fat of his old aunts, and had preferred clean silhouettes, long slim legs, soft, flat stomachs and small but firm breasts and firm and energetic bodies was happy as a clam at high tide in the profusion of flaccid flesh that she offered with such generosity. He sank into it with mad delight, transported by the ebb and flow of the spongy rolls where his entire being bathed in newfound ecstasy. Under the clothes that he modestly painted, he imagined the thighs spread out on the sheet, the fiery tuft and its full-bodied aroma, the perfect symmetry of the pubis, the generous folds of the belly under the heavy, tender breasts he hungrily kissed.

One day she came to see his finished work, and exclaimed furiously, 'Who is this fat woman? Is this a joke, son of a bitch! Must be your mother, this huge woman!' Another day, she asked to pose 'like in *Titanic*'. Even in the furthest corners of the old city, nobody had missed the film, especially the scene where the actress posed naked on a sofa for her handsome adventurer.

'Impossible,' Shanwaz replied.

She insisted.

'I don't have a sofa,' he hedged.

She persisted in her demand. Shanwaz, already under scrutiny from the fundamentalists who were always on the lookout for an excuse to declare a *fatwa* on him, knew it was impossible for him to even imagine making women pose naked for him at a stone's throw from one of Islam's most sacred places. She was cross with him for days and refused to open her screen door when he stood there pleading with her. He was finally obliged to give in but asked to make the portrait from memory. It was his first and only nude and he was so scared somebody would come across it that he didn't know where to hide it.

One sluggish spring afternoon, she convinced him to take her to his house. He had to give in once again. On the last floor he had converted one of the rooms attached to the apartment into a guest room where nobody ever went. A second door gave onto an independent staircase. While the three girls were at school, Sana had decided to hop over to meet her father, Mustafa – old and bedridden, finishing his days in an old people's home. She would be back only at night.

The two lovers climbed the spiral staircase as discreetly as possible and locked themselves into the room where Shanwaz had stocked some bottles of whisky. Procuring such drinks in a country where alcohol was prohibited since Bhutto's time was an exploit in itself. It was Taraq, his Christian servant, who helped Shanwaz get his stock from the city's international hotels. And Surayya had a little something in her small bag to reach an artificial paradise for ages. A little air blew in through the bay windows, easing the stuffy June heat. The sun filtered through the coloured glass windows, filling the room with a light that harked to his childhood days when the floor was left awash with yellows and oranges.

First they collapsed on the bed and took a good swig of whisky, nervously puffing at the cigarette to quash the dull dread of knowing that the family was so close. The alcohol and drugs induced an insane desire in Shanwaz. He did away with the erotic preliminaries, usually something that got all his attention, undressed and then helped Surayya get out of her clothes. The enormous musky mass stopped him in his tracks. Love was a strange thing. How could he express the force, the erotic attraction of such a body, he wondered, before delightfully ravaging the soft, torrid magma, losing his slim body in a stream of chubbiness and rippling curves like waves of barely-cooled lava. He trailed his penis, as hard as a bamboo under a fiery sun, in the hollows of the giant furrows. He grabbed the rolls of fat in his hands, pleasured just by touching the luxurious matter and sculpting it as he wanted, making soft cavities in it where his penis could abandon itself in a divine dance, a jubilation he had never known. I love you, he told her in silence, his eyes ecstatic with passion. Pore by pore, his greedy tongue licked every salty drop that ran down the bumpy lines like music on a stormy river. Her spongy body was sensuous. Rays of light fell on her soft, firm skin resembling a ripe, juicy fruit, and played on the transparent wet breasts swollen with tenderness. Surayya's fingers ran up the insides of his thighs, to his stomach and then down again to his pubic hair. He shivered under her caresses and moaned weakly in rhythm with the ice cream seller's cry. In his head, his mother's cries from the other side of the wall, Laila's sighs when their bodies separated, and Surayya's sighs in the stained folds of the sheet were all jumbled up. He was losing himself in the wisps of air saturated with exquisite, dizzying and unforgettably intoxicating odours of bitter-sweet, musky, opiated exhalations. The body under him moved with the grace of a primitive goddess and he floated on its overwhelming generosity, trembling with immeasurable pleasure. As he neared his climax, he gathered up the two separated breasts into a mound and caressed the two vibrating points with the tips of his fingers while he slipped his penis into the silky folds of her flesh. Surayya, her head deep in the pillows, hair spread out, eyes closed and mouth wide open, was swooning and groaning deeply. Shanwaz's pleasure doubled on seeing hers and he pressed the two breasts closer and closer together on the verge of ecstasy. Then he closed his eyes and came in one wet burst that dribbled down Surayya's neck.

Intoxicated by the fumes of alcohol and drugs, they lost track of time in their lust for each other and continued their games in the dimming light. Suddenly, a scream from behind the apartment door pulled them out of their reverie. For a while Shanwaz, who was on another planet, couldn't recognize Sana's voice. He sat up slowly, short of breath and bleary-eyed. He was on the edge of the bed, naked as a baby and sweating profusely, distractedly listening to the scream loud enough to wake the entire neighbourhood. Then he came to his senses and jumped to his feet and, panic-stricken, began to look for something to wear. The absurdity of the situation began to dawn on the odalisque-like Surayya lying on the dishevelled bed, and she burst out into uncontrollable laughter, her entire body rippling rebelliously. A distraught Shanwaz tried in vain to force her to dress. In the midst of all the confusion, Sana continued to batter the apartment door while little fists hammered the staircase door. There was no escape. On one side there was his wife, on the other his daughters. Once they had dressed, the two shabby lovers with their foul breaths and damp skin, their bodies stinking of semen, took the staircase door, preferring to avoid Sana.

If the girls were shocked at seeing their father come out looking like the devil, it was nothing compared to their stupefaction on seeing the gargantuan shrew who rapidly staggered down the stairs after him despite her size. Shanwaz appeared shameful and sheepish in front of his wife, his head all cloudy and throbbing like ten drums resonating inside, while she continued to scream that her life was over, that shame and dishonour had befallen her. She had seen everything through the cracks in the door, she whined.

Once the crisis had passed, she slipped into the bed she had deserted after the regrettable incident, and in a barely audible voice asked her husband if he could do with her what he had done with his mistress.

Her face still bore some traces of her youth, but her increasingly ungainly, ungraceful and obese body gave her much pain. Surayya, who was always ready to exchange reality for illusion, waited anxiously for Shanwaz's verdict after three days of fasting.

'Look, don't you think I'm thinner? Look at my hips, aren't they slimmer?'

And he acquiesced before the pathetic parody that her stomach was flatter and that it accentuated her breasts. He told her to not worry, that her beauty was luminous and her body desirable. Why did she torture herself so?

But it was the medicines that had really been troubling Shanwaz for some time. As soon as she had problems, Surayya swallowed a bunch of sleeping pills which she mixed with the drugs she could find as easily as bread in the neighbourhood. Hard drugs, the bad quality, tampered ones reserved for the poorest, diluted with toxic products that permanently messed up the neurons. Shanwaz sometimes wondered how she was still alive. What mysterious force lent this guileless halo to her face? So much tenderness hurriedly enveloped in a bundle of suffering.

He had very little influence over her. Only his presence soothed her. She came out of her hell and applied some kohl and lipstick to please him. Often her eyelids were so heavy with tears they wouldn't open to display what was left of the extraordinary green waters that still made her lover go weak in the knees. Shanwaz knew that she returned to her poisonous cocktails as soon as he left her, until the next coma. She wouldn't understand that it was impossible for him to stay with her on her second floor apartment. She wanted him all to herself, and yelled that he didn't love her like he said he did, that she could become his second wife, that he had the right to marry her. He tried to explain to her that he would never take a second wife. He could not bear to hurt the mother of his children.

'I am a human being first, then a Muslim.'

One night Surayya succumbed to an overdose.

14

An unusual sight on the roof of the house brought the curious neighbours out. On the surrounding terraces, clusters of children shoved and pushed in amusement, while modestly draped women looked on at the strangers placing strange objects everywhere. A radiant orange globe was smouldering in the deep abyss of the sky; the American TV crew from NBC was waiting for dusk to start the interview. The journalist in a blue shirt sat facing Shanwaz Nadeem in a black polo shirt. A chubby assistant had just placed lapel microphones on their collars while the cameraman made last minute adjustments for the dimming early-September light.

A year after the fatal New York tragedy, American TV channels were competing with each other to find original ideas to commemorate an event that had been exhausted of all representation over the past year. The NBC journalist was not unhappy with his find. It was an article published in the *Time* magazine that had brought him here to Lahore to meet this unusual and brazenly defiant personality in a country whose religious fanaticism was raising hackles in the West. General Pervez Musharraf had barely come into power before appearing on TV screens to declare: 'There will be democracy, but it will be our *own* democracy,' even as he appeased religious fundamentalists. The assassination of an American journalist by an Islamic nexus linked to Osama Bin Laden had contributed to the dramatic deterioration of Pakistan's reputation. Since then, any foreign media that ventured there were immediately suspected by the authorities of spying, and were closely watched during their work. Three Pakistanis in white shirts and impeccable jeans absently loitered on the terrace, listening in on the slightest conversation of the American team, sifting through every word uttered by the interviewee.

As he waited tensely on his chair for the first question, Shanwaz suddenly felt a puny little hand close around his in a feeble grasp. And the gentle pressure went straight to his heart. His son, Jamil, had hidden behind the heavy wrought-iron chairs, and reached out to hold his father's hand. His small head looked up and his sparkling eyes observed the strange bustle around him. Shanwaz had never loved Sana. She had never understood anything of his paintings, or of his desire to make something of himself. For years, she had done nothing but discourage him. In the mornings, when he came up from his workshop where he had been painting since dawn, he barely stepped onto the threshold before she set on him with her daily complaints about the lack of bread, or of money for this or for that, perpetually dissatisfied behind her myopic glasses which made her even uglier. This woman never saw the energy he put into trying to make a living for his family, his mother, and a few prostitutes living in misery, all these mouths to feed, and him alone, so alone that his loneliness gave him nightmares and he sometimes wanted to end it all. And recently it came so often that during his insomnia, he would prepare his will in his head – the house for his son, the paintings for the girls...and yes, a little something for this stranger he had spent every morning with for so many years, who never thought of greeting him or even preparing a cup of tea for him. Yes, a little something for her, so she wouldn't rot in misery like so many before her. A small little something to thank her for finally having given him what he had longed for – a son. A little boy who quickly became the puny god and undisputed tyrant of the house. Shanwaz found strength in the incomparable joy the child brought him, and swore to himself to give to his only son all that he had ever dreamed of.

The blinding sliver of a bright new moon appeared in the navy blue sky, but was quickly dimmed when the Badshahi and the fort were lit up. The monuments were enticingly aglow with the thousands of lamps that filled the twilight. It was a mesmerizing scene from the terrace. The perfect moment to film. Shanwaz sat on a chair, perspiring, his hands folded on the glass table that separated him from the journalist. The monsoon humidity hadn't left the intense evening heat. The assistant mopped his face with a paper towel.

His nervousness evaporated with the first question as his loud voice rang out. At sixty-five, Shanwaz feared no one and nothing. He was aware of what he had achieved and of the spectacular success of his life in this world he had never shied away from, a world he had looked in the eye and then built into a work of art. He was no longer ashamed of his origins, and he did not hesitate to talk about this unmentionable, endangered world. He talked about how one of Lahore's most legendary neighbourhoods had almost disappeared. Its culture, its traditions, its architecture, everything that made it unique in a Pakistan wilting under the weight of misery and intolerance, were on the verge of disappearing. Hira Mandi had radically changed over the past years. The police was on a clean-up drive, sneaking in at night into the four streets exclusively reserved for dancing and taking rich young papa's boys from the new city in for questioning, confiscating their identity cards and contacting their parents, scaring away the best clients.

Asif Sahudiqi had played turncoat. Benazir's failure also provoked his own fall, so he decided to drop politics and divorced his troublesome wife to devote himself to the promotion of young feminine talent. Every night his haveli was open to adolescents who dreamed of becoming stars. Alcohol and drugs made the rounds aplenty during the torrid evenings. Under his garb of the liberal-minded prince, he bribed the Shahi Mohalla police for his dirty work, particularly during the elections when the government needed to placate the mullahs without whom the military could not impose its dictatorship. Violent raids would be carried out and dancers stuffed into vans, then thrown into prison, and Asif would send his men to free them. In so becoming their saviour, he made them pay heavily for his alleged protection. Unable to stop the rot, the dancers began to abandon Hira Mandi. Many tried to get visas for Dubai through the vast networks of people always on the lookout for women and alcohol. Those that remained lapsed into desuetude. The girls no longer came from families claiming Mughal lineage, but from the villages of the Punjab. Miserable peasant women in search of glamour who had learned to dance by watching Indian films, stuffed into a salon with the twanging tones of some music blaring from a radio that replaced musicians. Garish make up distorted their cherubic faces, and the junk jewellery that decorated their gaudy shalwar kameez replaced the elegant with the grotesque as a seduction tool. Even the men had changed – they were harsh, vulgar and didn't give a fig for dance, they only wanted quick release within the hour.

And thus the tradition of grand Mughal courtesans was lost to sordid prostitution.

The journalist signalled to the cameraman to stop filming. Like Shanwaz, he too was dripping with sweat. Armed with a box of paper towels, the assistant mopped the two men. The sultry heat was stifling, with not a wisp of air to dispel the humidity that clung to the skin. After a short break, Shanwaz continued his story for the fascinated journalist with his ever-unsmiling face thrown into relief by a projector.

In Shahi Mohalla, everything was linked – politics and religion, sexual repression and cruelty, music and misery, lost children and battered women, rotting lepers and emaciated drug addicts, all flowed in one illogical tide of ideas and cultures. With no justice. Which was why the populace remained so attached to the PPP, a party that had always known tragedy with leaders like Bhutto and his daughter, and with whom the city empathized. These politicians knew perfectly well how to play with the feelings and suffering of the inhabitants of the old city. At the dawn of the twenty-first century, there were still no schools or doctors or hospitals behind these walls. Just rot. In all his life in Hira Mandi, Shanwaz had never seen any representative from any government come enquire about the plight of the people in this neighbourhood. Nothing, ever. No one. Even Asif Sahudiqi, when he became minister, would leave his haveli in the mornings and come back only in the evenings, more concerned about his worldly parties than the gutters overflowing with misery.

This was why Shanwaz had started painting. Not to please or to create art for art's sake, beauty for beauty's sake, but to reveal the misery of his neighbourhood and these women excluded from society. He had painted them without pathos or glamour, in their disturbing reality. 'I belong to this world, I can see its reality from within and that is exactly what I want to show in my paintings,' he had repeated for years. And how happy it made him when his paintings touched people and left them overwhelmed or in a state of shock! Art should shake things up, intoxicate to the point of monopolizing the mind for a long time.

'My country should be proud of me, instead it scorns me, threatens me and wants to be rid of me. But I am certain that the culture and traditions of Shahi Mohalla will live on through my paintings, like XVIth century Italian society lives on through the canvasses of Renaissance painters. I share my passion for painting with artists who, like me, paint with their guts, their emotions, their feelings. I have become a great painter, Pakistan's most famous, my work is exhibited in the East and the West but in my own country, my paintings disturb people. What I want to show through the misery of the perpetually repressed woman, is the agony of a state that has been looking for its way for fifty years and hasn't found it.'

The NBC journalist often brought up the question of the risks that he took and the danger he faced in a country of emerging religious fundamentalism. Without batting an eyelid in front of the camera, Shanwaz repeated that mullahs regularly came by to ask if he was a good Muslim, urging him – with a finger raised to the sky – to not shock his brothers with his offensive representations. None had come into his restaurant and seen the many statues of Hindu gods and a Christ on a crucifix, and the large bust of a naked woman originally from Afghanistan.

'With figures like this in my house, in a public place a stone's throw from a place as sacred as the Badshahi, I risk death.'

He then turned his face towards the mosque, and a rebellious smile lit up his face.

He hadn't told the intrusive camera what he concealed deep within him, his dreams, his precious secrets. The dream of buying a house overlooking the little square from his childhood so that the prostitutes would no longer need to pay for water or electricity, so they could break free from erring men who were here a while, then elsewhere with other women, leaving fatherless children in their wake. The dream of giving life to the courtesans' neighbourhood again and redoing the salons for real dancers who could revive Mughal traditions. The dream of seeing beautiful crafts shops and art galleries around his house, elegant cafés inside the beautiful Mughal buildings. But the mullahs condemned him for promoting prostitution and the police condemned him for denouncing their brutality towards the girls.

15

Sitting in the back of the room on one of the wooden seats buffed by many a fidgety posterior, Shanwaz was losing himself in the depths of Nusrat Fateh Ali Khan's impelling voice. The walls of the City Cinema were struggling to contain the jostling crowd that had formed in front of the locked doors as soon as the sun went down. The reigning star of Qawwali had taken his time but, finally, at one in the morning, the entire Khan family had descended on the dozing room – the musician cousins, the uncle who replaced the defunct father, and Nusrat. Obese and ill, Pakistan's most cherished singer had hesitantly walked towards the stage, almost staggering, a man weighed down by the size of his own frame. He had to be helped up the few steps to the stage. The crowds launched into delirious clapping and screaming when he appeared. In the balcony, the younger generations went wild, and stamped the floor with their feet. For several long minutes, while the group settled in on a carpet laid out on the middle of the stage, the deafening chorus of enthusiastic fans filled the auditorium. But when the tabla started, a hush fell in an instant. Then the notes of the harmonium rose into the beams of multicoloured lights. For a long while, the music soared like the translucent wings of a bird, then the ardent voice of the man sitting cross-legged in the midst of the musicians cut through the disconcerting caress of the night with nuanced simplicity. Nusrat, the half-angel, half-demon Sufi Buddha, had launched into his hypnotic rhythmic singing. His unrelenting breath took his voice higher and higher into the heavens with the luminous fervour of a priest delivering a spiritual message.

Shanwaz closed his eyes and allowed himself to be transported by waves of infinite dimensions. Enveloped in the music, he saw the past years flash before his eyes, ecstatic mobs cheering 'Zia is dead! Zia is dead!' a cry that was repeated for days afterwards, like a cathartic prayer. The news had spread across the country faster than flood water in the streets. In Lahore, the populace had cleaned out the sweet shops like they did during festivals. The dictator's death was a terrifying example of divine retribution. On 17 August 1988 his plane had crashed while returning from the Bhawalpur military base and it had burned for five hours. People believed that Zia had so misused Islam that God had wanted to wipe out all signs of him. It had not been possible to perform the last rites of washing the body and turning the head towards Mecca. The coffin buried in the Shah Faisal mosque in Islamabad didn't contain any part of him. On that day, the sky had unleashed a shower that had washed the land clean. Devastating floods hit a Lahore suburb, and swept away houses and livestock without warning. The waters brought down walls, washed away roads and broke tombs in the cemeteries. There was widespread indignation when it was learned that an embankment that protected a very poor, over-populated area from floods had deliberately been blown up by Zia's regional administration to protect affluent residential areas. The waters rose and cut the city off for over two weeks. Thousands of people lost all they owned. But after so many years of torment, hope rose again a few months later with the election of the Bhutto goddess. She was, after her father, the second prime minister in the history of the country to be elected by the people. But the Benazir for whom all of Hira Mandi had voted and for whom all its inhabitants would have gladly jumped into a fire, that Benazir had not risked lifting the heavy cotton curtains whose absence would have allowed the backward, the underprivileged and the tramps to enjoy the houris in Allah's paradise; instead she had confined them to the belief according to the Prophet that 'a race will never prosper if authority lies in the hands of a woman'. It had taken only two years for the virtuous to oust the one adored by the streets. After forty years of cynicism and intellectual sloth, the State, once equated with God, had become a corrupt criminal system. In this violent country, coup d'états and earth quakes followed one after the other at a dramatic rate. Nawaz Sharif had taken over the seat left vacant for two years, then Benazir had come back for two short years before being sent into exile, while her husband, nicknamed 'Mister ten percent', was thrown into jail for many long years.

The entire room held its breath in transports of delight at Nusrat's dazzling voice. Under the single beam of light that shone on him, he seemed to float above the floor. The increasingly frenzied musicians around him perspired in a space that seemed to have been emptied of all air. Shanwaz, sweating buckets in his seat, on another trip down memory lane, lost himself in the watery green eyes of the only woman who had effaced his memories of Laila. Surayya: the captivating female with mystical powers, the dancer whose conspirational grace dragged men into bewitching abysses. Surayya, the obese courtesan of inexplicable beauty who would open her monumental thighs for him and take him on a joyride through his humid agony. He would end the allegorical marathon short of breath, his senses heightened, his body covered in lustral water. His happiness melted into a dream of pure contentment, a doomed but extraordinarily strong life force. After her death, he had stayed in his workshop with his sorrow, in front of the portraits laid down like offerings at his feet, with the misty whisky to fill his loneliness with despair. With the second glass, his life changed direction. The air became sweet like honey and sugar. He would stay there for hours in a feverish silence regularly tainted by the shrill noises of the rickshaws, wondering where this life so afflicted by disasters was headed.

After Surayya's death, he had suffered seeing his daughter Aisha on her deathbed in front of Naseem whose visceral selfishness had made her push her granddaughter's promising future into the worst existence possible. She had vehemently opposed Aisha's entry into films, convinced that it was high time she had children. And what better father for her first child than the rich Asif Sahudiqi? Benazir's rise to power had given succour to his career too, and the fervent advocate of the PPP had re-joined the ranks in the hopes of seeing his pugnacity rewarded by a ministerial job. He needed a slick reputation as an honest supporter to get Benazir's attention. Under the repeated instigations of her grandmother, the young dancer besotted with the handsome Hira Mandi aristocrat was trying to get pregnant by him. But Naseem's plans were foiled by Asif's ambitious and prodigious leap to the nation's higher echelons with the faithful amongst the faithful. In one magical moment he was showered with the privileges of a ministerial post, and he walked all over the obsequious bureaucrats lined up before him the minute he entered his ministerial office.

For a more dignified career, he sent Aisha home and took a wife. Aisha never got to see his ambitious project come into being. A sumptuous woman with a long mane of black hair found amongst Benazir's most ardent followers officially took her place and changed things around at the Barood Khana. There was no question any longer of having dancers with dubious reputations, only exemplary wives accompanied by their equally exemplary husbands. One could catch fleeting glimpses of stars at their lavish parties, such as the recent cricket world champion with young London models on his arms.

Aisha went back to Hira Mandi's harsh universe and her small salon, and the clients trooped in again, one of whom would be the anonymous father of her first child. A boy. But to Naseem's great relief, the child died of a treacherous draught of air. Aisha's beauty wilted under the repeated tragedies that befell her, and she lost the radiance she had exuded over Asif's guests during her real but transient glory years. She became pregnant again. The pregnancy started well enough, then one night she felt a peculiar pain that brought on an inexplicable fever. Nobody bothered to call a doctor, and Naseem put it down to the usual discomforts of pregnancy. Then one night she found Aisha almost dead on sheets wet with water and blood. The doctor who finally examined her diagnosed a generalized infection caused by the foetus that had died several weeks ago.

A shadow of her former self, Aisha left with it. After that, Naseem didn't utter another word. Loyally dressed in black, she would sit on the little balcony in her room, and stare listlessly at the Badshahi from dawn to dusk. Surprised by the violence of his feelings, Shanwaz opened his eyes to Nusrat's round face, his heart-rending deep voice accompanied by two tiny hands like two puppets in the air on colossal arms, the hands of a drowning man, reaching out to an intangible divinity in a frenzied room lit with crackling lamps. 'Reject your heart, it's a slave to reason,' sang the chorus around Nusrat. The singer's feverish eyes were bright with devotion. His voice came from the depths of his soul, swelling and floating above the ebbing and flowing waves of music.

Shanwaz remembered the infamous book that had inflamed public opinion and stirred an Islamic controversy. Ignorance had fuelled minds eager for obscenity. *The Satanic Verses* had attracted the wrath of hell and Rushdie became Satan personified, 'reduced to vagabondage and chaotic wandering'. Book-burning was the order of the day across the country, although nobody had ever even opened the book. Rushdie was hated doubly because of his Indian origins, and when the *fatwa* was declared on him, he was thrown into a world without a motherland in the name of a religion that believed it had been denigrated.

For a long time, the story oppressed the air around the Badshahi, where fundamentalists met to cleanse their souls of the impious insult and the contamination by the depraved, so that Allah in his infinite purity could regain his majesty. Groups of them decided to declare war on those they saw as disrespectful of the precepts of the Quran. Shanwaz was one of their favourite targets, and he never forgot their faces, hidden under their beards thick as bramble bushes, the day they encroached on his doorstep, belching words from their diseased minds, articulating barely-veiled death-threats. But Shanwaz didn't give in. He didn't want fear to weaken his resolve. He was determined to fight forever against injustice, lies and irrationality, and he would not let anything get in his way, not their obsession for revenge or the cruelty in their eyes that saw him as a lost soul. He would never be a slave to this religion peppered with fanatics. Never give in to the brutal childishness which drove them mad with loathing at the idea of a woman and her imagined pleasure.

For Shanwaz, woman was God's most beautiful creation in this obscure world. When he lost everything, after the last flames had licked at the skies, it was the starry eyes of a dancer that still distracted him. Devastated by his life's vision reduced to ashes and smoke, he thought of love, and the two times in his life that his heart had lived. His raison d'être.

In one last flourish, Nusrat's voice entered the intimate euphoria of a fiery public that sensed the end of the concert after two hours in a trance. Men stood up, stamping their feet, clapping their hands to the rhythm of the last notes. When the musicians finished, reality took over again. Outside, dawn was whitening the sky.

Alone in the dark room, his head resting on the edge of the seat, Shanwaz stared, unmoving, at the ceiling with his eyes wide open. He had nothing left. Just some dreams. But nobody to share them with.

He climbed up to the terrace, where he often found refuge when Lahore's lights went out and all that remained in the sky was an ashen disk. He liked the hours that led to the dawn, those surreal, satanic moments when silence took over the world.

He would sit down facing the stars, uncork his flask of whisky and pursue his ultimate dream with singular intensity – Laila, her perfect beauty, her tender lips, her hair that smelled of jasmine, her body ready for love. But before he could let her come closer, he had to make her drink so that in her inebriated state she could forget his advanced years and caress his old withered body without revulsion.